UNDERCURRENTS   Series Editor Carol Coulter

Understanding Corruption in Irish Politics

NEIL COLLINS AND
MARY O'SHEA

CORK **cup** UNIVERSITY PRESS

First published in 2000 by
Cork University Press
University College
Cork
Ireland

British Library Cataloguing in Publication Data
A CIP catalogue record for this book is available from
the British Library

ISBN 1 85918 273 9

Typeset by Tower Books, Ballincollig, Co. Cork
Printed by ColourBooks, Baldoyle, Co. Dublin

UNDERCURRENTS

Understanding Corruption in Irish Politics

UNDERCURRENTS

Other titles in the series

Contents

Introduction

Mary McAleese, President of Ireland, spoke for the majority when she said that the 'sordid side of the country's secret life is now under the spotlight and we are deeply challenged by the evidence of many different forms of corruption' (*The Irish Times*, 12.6.00). Corruption in political and business life in particular has become the most prominent issue in the Republic of Ireland today. A *Sunday Tribune* (9.7.00) opinion poll placed corruption in business and politics as the most salient issue for the electorate of the Republic. The public's view clearly reflects the impact of the tribunals and inquiries that have exposed corrupt practices in recent years. If corruption remains the top priority for voters by the time the next election comes around, it will have a profound impact on the outcome.

To understand political corruption in Ireland, it is necessary to examine the concept within an analytical framework that allows both historical and international comparison. Attention to the daily media narrative alone presents the danger that Ireland's current experience could be seen as more serious and widespread than it is.

> The reminder that corruption exists everywhere, in private as well as public sectors, in rich countries and poor, is salutary, because it helps us avoid unhelpful stereotypes. . . . [But] noting that corruption is widespread may convey its own unhelpful subliminal messages. It may suggest . . . that all forms and instances of corruption are equally harmful . . . [or that] nothing can be done about it here. Consider the analogy of pollution or disease. Both exist everywhere on the planet. But the extent and patterns differ radically across settings. With disease, questions of degree and kind are crucial, and so is the case with corruption.[1]

Definitions of corruption are broad ranging. Some authors opt for definitions based on laws and other formal rules because these allow relative precision and stability. Others stress cultural standards to accommodate more realistic and subtle definitions. A third school seeks to put the wider political implications of corruption and the moral issues centre stage.[2] An accepted core element, which is taken here as a working definition, is 'the abuse of public office for private gain'. Such gain is not necessarily financial but is of personal or partisan value to those involved.

The heightened public and media interest in political corruption in Ireland is mirrored in the attention paid to it internationally. The academic literature is vast and, in the main, relatively recent. In part, this research resource has been encouraged by international bodies, notably the World Bank and the OECD, and specialist non-governmental organisations, such as Transparency International. There has been a growing realisation that corruption undermines economic growth most markedly in developing countries. Foreign investment is discouraged by corruption and the effectiveness of foreign aid is reduced. Donor nations are increasingly reticent about giving to political systems in which corrupt local politicians and officials routinely divert money. Perhaps as a result, several developing countries, notably Lesotho and its African neighbours, have recently initiated major anti-corruption strategies.

This reassessment of the importance of corruption in developing countries has led to the development of new analytical models that facilitate comparison. This book presents some of these academic constructs as a counter to the descriptive assessments that dominate the discourse on corruption in Ireland. It also seeks to refute the idea, often found in media coverage, that the Republic has joined the ranks of irredeemably base regimes. For example, the *Sunday Times* (23.7.00) claimed that '. . . when it comes to bribery and corruption Irish politicians have nothing to learn from African dictators'. If such assessments are allowed to gain currency unchallenged, Ireland will neither be able to understand its corruption nor to counter it intelligently.

Neil Collins and Mary O'Shea
June 2000

1. Understanding Corruption in Irish Politics

To analyse corruption in an Irish context, it is useful to appreci-
ate how it is understood in the broader academic literature. It is
also important to move beyond the simple image of giving and
receiving bribes or 'brown envelopes' in return for particular
favours. Corruption is not confined to single transactions. In
many circumstances, it is part of an ongoing routine in which
those with public responsibilities extract personal benefit above
their official pay.

Similarly, corrupt activity is often described using the idea of
'rent seeking' that derives from economics.[1] Rent, for economists, is earnings above market returns including all relevant
costs. It is equivalent, in everyday terms, to monopoly profit.
The idea of rent seeking is critical to the neoliberal school of
Public Choice, currently a very influential perspective in public
policy making. The theory explains almost all situations in
which there is scarcity arising from a lack of perfect competition. Whenever the state intervenes to control the market
through regulations, licences, quotas or direct provision of services it creates rent-seeking opportunities.

'Corruption is made possible by a discretional use of power
not anticipated by the rules.'[2] In the context of corruption, therefore, rent seeking is looking for opportunities to acquire an extra
return which, for public officials or politicians, is outside their
legitimate reward.

> Arguments advanced take it as axiomatic that...govern-
> mental organization is 'bogged' down in a welter of
> uncoordinated, undirected, ambivalent, mutually
> antagonistic and contradictory objectives . . . that make
> it a prey to manipulation by every lobby and corrupting
> agent.[3]

The actions of corrupt politicians and officials imply an abuse
of trust though economists seldom use that concept. Indeed,
some see corruption as an extension of the economics of crime

in which actions are solely governed by a utilitarian calculation of costs and benefits. The amount and impact of corruption is governed by supply and demand with a tendency to seek an equilibrium price.

> The shortcomings in the constancy of references to the economies of crime is the distant image of the reality of a flexible and pareto-optimum equilibrium price in terms of which the corrupt transaction is effected. Hence the compulsion both to reduce economic agents to an individual maximizing unit and to maintain the assumption of rational calculation on the part of this unit ruin the economies of criminal corruption as projected. Certainly society is far from being a continuum of pure and perfect markets.[4]

The value of the economics-based concept is in the focus it gives to the circumstances that give rise to the potential for rent as well as the institutions or policies that militate against it. In particular, economists recommend structures that reduce rent-enhancing elements of discretion in the supply of public services or elements of monopoly control.

Economists make substantial claims for their perspective.

> Economics is a powerful tool for the analysis of corruption. Cultural differences and morality provide nuance and subtlety, but an economic approach is fundamental to understanding where corrupt incentives are the greatest and have the biggest impact.[5]

Couching an analysis of political corruption in market-based terms should, however, also alert the observer to the limits of economic models of politics and public management. Patterns of behaviour that may be acceptable in the private sector are outside accepted limits for those charged with the public interest. Citizens may expect higher standards than customers even in the context of public sector reforms that seek to introduce business practices to the machinery of government. The economists' certainties are based on the simple assumption that a narrow understanding of self-interest motivates all actors. It discounts any democratic or public service motive.

While economists such as Klitgaard are very influential globally in the analysis of corruption, other approaches also provide useful insights. Sociologists, for example, also see corruption as crime but focus on the different response to it from the state when contrasted to violent or property offences. They focus on social control, i.e. collective efforts to ensure conformity to social norms and expectations. A distinction is made between informal and formal social control. The former includes the norms of family and community life that individuals learn while young. Formal social control is the enforcement of conformity through legal and other institutions. Rapid economic development can weaken informal social controls and lead to rising crime.

From the perspective of neo-Marxist sociologists a central concept is 'hegemony', a term used by Gramsci (1891–1937) to analyse the modern capitalist state's manoeuvres to maintain its hegemonic position.[6] Gramsci argues that the capitalist state cannot simply rely on coercion to survive. It needs the consent of the dominated classes by presenting itself as the guardian of common interests. Although its central function is to defend the interest of the capitalist class, the state has constantly to adjust its policies with reference to wider class interests and power relationships. Government actions against corruption are, therefore, calculated to deflect the discontent of majority onto a few scapegoats while still tolerating corruption, the crime of the rich and influential. Ironically, from this perspective, the more dramatic and publicised the disgrace of the few 'big fish', the better the state may be protecting capitalist interests. An assuaged public opinion restores the hegemony of the capitalist class as a whole.

Another interesting perspective is provided by anthropology. An Indian social anthropologist, Prakash Reddy, studying a village in Denmark, observed that:

> . . . the villagers hardly knew one another. They rarely
> exchanged visits and had few other social contacts.
> They had little information on what other villagers . . .
> were doing and . . . little interest . . . Even . . . parents
> and children were not very close. When the children
> reached adulthood they moved out and, after that, they
> visited their parents only occasionally.[7]

By contrast in a typical Indian village of comparable size everybody showed an active interest in their family and neighbours. They visited each other frequently especially the extended families. Villagers would support each other on many levels.

Denmark and India may represent opposite ends of a continuum but the villages provide interesting touchstones. Corruption, as defined here, would be much less likely to prevail in the Danish village than in the Indian village. In the latter, treating your family and neighbours other than preferentially:

> . . . would seem strange and alien. It would even seem
> immoral. The idea that, economically speaking, one
> should treat relatives and friends in the same way as
> strangers would appear bizarre. Relatives and friends
> would simply expect preferential treatment whether
> they were dealing with individuals in the private or in
> the public sphere . . . Many developing countries would
> probably be closer to the model represented by the
> Indian village. Some industrial countries, such as Italy
> and possibly Japan, would also come closer to the latter
> than the former.[8]

Ironically, the factors that make a country a less cold and indifferent place may also be inappropriate in the modern state.

Categorisations of corruption are numerous but, following Robinson (1998), the three main forms are incidental (individual), institutional and systemic or societal (see Table 1.1) Thus, in some political systems, corruption may only involve the occasional 'rogue' politician or official and be episodic rather than sustained.

TABLE 1.1: Types of Corruption

1–INCIDENTAL
– Small-scale;
– involving individual and junior public officials such as policemen, customs and tax officials;
– Little macro-economic cost, but profound public alienation;
– Often hard to curb.
2–INSTITUTIONAL
– Larger development impact;
– Can affect most or all of a government department, or a parastatal such as procurement agency or marketing board;
– Can have substantial impact upon government revenues and trade diversion;
– Sustained reform effort necessary rather than 'individualised' response
3–SYSTEMIC
– Wholly corrupt system;
– Huge development impact;
– In such circumstances, honesty is 'irrational';
– Reform by fundamental change?

Source: Riley, S.P., 'The Political Economy of Anti–Corruption Strategies in Africa', in M. Robinson (ed.) *Corruption and Development* (London: Frank Cass,1998)

> Incidental corruption is small-scale corruption and usually involves isolated individuals or small numbers of individuals: very junior public officials . . . This petty corruption does not have macro-economic impact but can be profoundly alienating to the public: as citizens and as consumers of public resources. Incidental corruption is also often hard to curb.[9]

In other cases, however, some central or local government departments or groups of elected officials might be routinely corrupt. Such corruption is referred to here as institutional but by Riley as systematic. It may be associated with one state function, a particular ministry or local authority. This institutional corruption may reflect the nature of their work or the laxity of control, auditing etc. Such corruption is isolated but persistent.

> . . . systematic [i.e. institutional] corruption . . . involves a larger number of public officials and an element of

> organisation and conspiracy . . . It is typically found in government departments or parastatals such as procurement agencies and marketing boards.[10]

It contrasts with the third category that covers the most extreme circumstances.

> Most systems can stand some corruption, and it is possible that some truly awful systems can be improved by it. But when corruption becomes the norm, its effects are crippling. So, although every country has corruption, the varieties and extent differ. The killer is systematic corruption that destroys the rules of the game. It is one of the principal reasons why the most underdeveloped parts of our planet stay that way.[11]

In these systemically corrupt political systems, some form of corruption taints almost all transactions. All state institutions, politicians and, probably, anyone in social authority will expect to make illicit private gains from official business. For example:

> Political corruption in Thailand has pervaded day-to-day existence where illegal exchanges of money affect transactions from the price of food to the provision of electricity in schools. Many Thai citizens believe that politicians rob them of their tax money for personal gain. Prevalent as well is vote buying during elections.[12]

Case studies from other jurisdictions suggest that systemic corruption is rare in liberal democracies. When the legitimacy of the government is not in question, property and contract rights are clear and the rule of law is broadly upheld; all-pervasive or systemic corruption is hard to sustain. This is particularly the case when changes of government do not threaten the whole political order. The more competitive economies associated with liberal democracies may also provide fewer rent-seeking opportunities for corrupt public figures than state-centred systems.

> All else equal, corruption can be expected to increase as the dependence of the private sector increases, as the number of interactions between business people and officials increases, and as intervention becomes more detailed and discretionary.[13]

The economic model is presaged on assumptions of rational self-interest. It anticipates behaviour accordingly.

> Corruption increases if the benefits expected from it are higher than the risk involved . . . As for government officials, they will be more inclined to accept bribes if they feel that their salaries or social status are inferior to their qualifications – especially when rewards in the private sector tend to be higher.[14]

That the poverty of officials in developing countries is an important factor can be gauged from a recent poll.

> [In a Transparency International survey] 65 per cent believed that low public sector salaries were the prime cause of corruption . . . About one third of those questioned were senior executives of international companies and one third were bankers, accountants, lawyers and heads of chambers of commerce. (*Financial Times*, 21.1.00)

In developed economies, it is not the practice to pay either politicians or public servants such low salaries that fraud or bribery is an 'accepted' form of income. Neither have public sector reforms in most countries significantly altered the security of tenure of public servants, the principle of merit recruitment or political accountability for policy. Thus, the conditions for systemic corruption are seldom present in the acute form that is reported in Africa and Latin America. As Geddes and Neto (1999) put it:

> Corrupt individuals can achieve power some proportion of the time in any political system, but some systems enhance both the usefulness of corruption to the

individual engaged in politics and their ability to get
away with corrupt practices while in office.[15]

Much of the literature on corruption is tutored by principal/agent theories. In these, the main actors are the politician or public official who is charged with public responsibilities, i.e. the agent (A), and the principal (P), i.e. the state or its citizens. As Heywood (1997) puts it: '. . . political corruption occurs when an agent breaks the law in sacrificing the interest of a principal to his or her own benefit.'[16]

Klitgaard introduces a third actor into this equation, the client (C). It is the client who is the corrupter and the agent who is corrupted. Thus, for illustration, a minister (A) may abuse the power given by the state (P) to award a contract to a political supporter (C) outside the established criteria. Acknowledging that the politician is often both a principal and an agent because, in day-to-day dealings, he or she defines the public interest, can usefully refine this P–A–C model. This model, taken from Galtung's account, can be represented by Table 1.2 .[17]

As Jain points out, however, not all rent seeking is corrupt.

> [The] process is recognised as free of corruption if all of
> the following three conditions are met.
>   1. It represents a competitive game played under
>   rules known to all players,
>   2. There are no secret or side payments to the agent,
>   and
>   3. The clients and the agents are independent of
>   each other in the sense that none of these benefits
>   from income earned by the other.
> If any of these three conditions is violated, the process
> acquires characteristics of corruption.[18]

Illustrations, such as those in Table 1.2, are problematic in that they presuppose a broader consensus about what corruption is than may exist in reality. It is clear that each country's legal norms, historical experience and cultural understandings influence definitions of corruption. Geddes and Neto draw on an

TABLE 1.2: Illustrative Categories of Corruption (and Fraud)

	P^1(STATE/CITIZEN)	P^2/A^1(POLITICIAN)	A^2(CIVIL SERVANT)	C
P^1	[No corruption]	–	–	–
P^2/A^1	Embezzlement Theft of public funds Vote rigging	Bribery Extortion		
A^2	Embezzlement Abuse of public goods	Personnel scams Internal pay-offs Corruption of internal investigations	Personnel scams Nepotism	
C	[Fraud] Tax evasion Public procurement cartels Illicit capital transfers	'Grand corruption' Extortion 'Collusion' Sale of public office Vote buying Illicit party funding Clientelism	Bribery Extortion 'Collusion' Facilitation payments Clientelism Backsheesh	[Private sector corruption]

Source: Galtung, F., 'Criteria for Sustainable Corruption Control' in M. Robinson (ed.), *Corruption and Development* (London: Frank Cass, 1998). pp.105–28

older understanding of American corruption, to include 'the exchange of resources for political support', while noting that in the Brazilian context of their study, this 'is often legal but violates norms of fairness and efficiency'.[19] They term this 'pork-barrel politics'.

An interesting boundary case found in Galtung is clientelism. In Ireland, there is an expectation that politicians will act on behalf of constituents looking for favourable treatment by public servants, especially when some ambiguity or grounds for discretion can be identified. This is referred to in the Irish context as clientelism, although it is more accurately brokerage. The key distinction is that the politician is dispersing state-owned benefits rather than personal largesse. Up to the early 1970s, for example, low-level public sector posts were awarded at the discretion of local politicians. Jobs as local authority rent collectors and manual workers could be 'found' using political influence. Similarly, transfers of staff within the Republic's police or prison services were the subject of political canvassing. These positions are no longer subject to either direct control or routine interference by politicians.

Various studies have described Irish politicians as specialists helping the bureaucratically illiterate'. The working class use the clientelist system most.[20] Cases of social welfare, housing and medical entitlements dominate parliamentary deputies' caseloads. These 'customer' complaints may not be heard if not facilitated by politicians. It is important to note that the evidence from case studies offers a picture of clientelism or brokerage that is low key and routine. Major allocative decisions are not at issue. The elector may or may not be accommodated, but the politician will feel that some electoral advantage has been gained from the exchange. No money or other inducement is involved. Still, some political cultures would focus on the 'apparent' privilege given to the citizen using a politician as opposed to the equally entitled direct applicant. Similarly, the advantages that are associated with having a minister as a constituency representative may be considered inappropriate elsewhere. As Garret FitzGerald, a former Taoiseach, put it:

> [There is an] expectation . . . that ministers will not merely ensure that particular problems relating to their area are borne in mind generally by government, but that their minister will deliver specific benefits to their constituency . . . Unhappily this expectation is often realised; pork-barrelling of this kind is a feature of the Irish governmental system. (*The Irish Times*, 1.3.97)

Even since FitzGerald made these comments, the benefits to some constituencies of a local minister have included the allocation of government offices under a decentralisation policy. Such localism is not specific to Ireland. Nevertheless, what in Ireland and elsewhere would be accepted as the normal and legitimate use of political representatives, especially at local level, may elsewhere be considered corrupt. In Britain, for example, politicians frequently see their role as resisting a localist perspective and, even at municipal level, policy discussion is dominated by a generalist and professional paradigm.

Italy 1992–4

> . . . while corruption is in no way limited to democracies, it is in such systems that its effects are most disruptive. By attacking two of the fundamental principles on which democracy is based, the equality of citizens before institutions and the open nature of decision making, corruption contributes to the delegitimation of the political and institutional systems in which it takes root.[21]

A reference point for corruption in a liberal democracy is the Italian case. In 1992 the Italian political system began to collapse amidst the scandals brought to light by the *mani pulite* (operation clean hands) investigations. Despite years of instability, the system had never seemed more secure. In November 1991, the Italian Socialist Party and the Christian Democrats had agreed to govern together for a further five years. The so-called *tangentopoli* scandal demonstrated that both corruption and organised crime had infiltrated Italian political life. Magistrates investigated hundreds of politicians and brought charges against many of them. The demise of the established political elite, the collapse of the long-standing governing parties and the undermining of many Cold War 'certainties' was signalled by the 1994 election that returned the coalition government headed by Silvio Berlusconi and his *Forza Italia* party. The investigation of corruption by magistrates is still continuing in Italy. Many of the lessons for Ireland, however, can be seen in events of 1992 to 1994.

Italian political corruption must be understood in a context of the traditional clientelism of Mediterranean states. As understood in Italy, clientelism and corruption are synonymous.

Clientelism and corruption converge to form a rising spiral, the diffusion of the one easing that of the other and vice versa.[22] Della Porta and Vannucci illustrate the vicious circle between clientelism and corruption in the following table:

TABLE 1.3: Vicious Circle between Clientelism and Corruption

Clientelism ⇒ increase of exchange votes ⇒ increase in the cost of politics ⇒ supply of corruption ⇒ availability of money for politicians ⇒ incentives to buy votes ⇒ clientelism

---

Politicians used public resources directly as a form of private asset in order to secure votes. The individual politician's clientelistic network needed to be broad and include both public institutions and private business interests. The network required to be continually maintained and widened to increase the scope for corrupt transactions. By increasing public expenditure on particular projects or departments, the politician augmented the potential of his or her network. The profits from corruption were invested in campaigning for re-election, funding a political faction or increasing the sphere of influence.

A clear example of this can be shown in the case of ATM, the municipal transport company in Milan and its largest publicly owned concern. It was shown to have been involved in large-scale bribery. Nevertheless, the company managers, who were politically appointed, appeared helpless in the face of this vast and organised system of corruption. In reality, as the *'mani pulite'* investigations revealed, they were party to it. While bribes on contracts under 100 million lira went to the managers, the politicians took a percentage on contracts above that amount.

The larger the coverage of a politician's network the less was the incentive for dissent. The public servants, who facilitated the politician, and business interests were profiting directly through bribes and indirectly by the electoral success of their patron. The 'kick-backs' to politicians were an 'investment' for the private businesses concerned. The losers were the Italian taxpayers.

The system of corruption in Italy was underpinned by a compliant public service. Even if contracts were awarded on an apparently competitive basis, extra costs, surcharges, surveys etc. were subsequently sanctioned. Alternatively, lower quality public works, poor services and late delivery were tolerated. Occasionally, 'phantom' public facilities were maintained via expensive service contracts. Poor public administration arose from corruption but it also facilitated it by providing the loopholes and official discretion that politicians exploited. Again, della Porta and Vannucci[23] point to a vicious circle. This vicious circle is as follows:

TABLE 1.4: Vicious Circle between Poor Administration and Corruption

Misadministration $\Rightarrow$ mistrust in implementation of citizens rights $\Rightarrow$ search for protection $\Rightarrow$ propensity for paying bribes $\Rightarrow$ (demand of) corruption $\Rightarrow$ selective inclusion $\Rightarrow$ increased (perception of) maladministration

The perception of poor administration encouraged citizens and business interests to pay bribes to secure speedier official procedures or the opportunity for contracts. The poor functioning of public administration generated widespread scepticism among citizens and entrepreneurs concerning the efficiency and impartiality of the procedures that regulated access to the state. One Sicilian politician observed:

> administrative paralysis transforms any right into a favour. If you need a certificate or a building permit and have to wait about two years to receive it, then you end up asking (and paying) for it as a favour. (*La Republica*, 17.10.91, quoted in della Porta and Vannucci, 1999: p. 58).

It is in the interests of corrupt politicians and civil servants to present the state as inefficient and unpredictable because:

> . . . then they can selectively offer protection from such inconveniences. In exchange for bribes they are willing

> to guarantee speedier consideration of particular cases, favourable interpretation of the regulations, simpler procedures or a positive outcome in clashes with the public administration.[24]

The role of the Mafia in some individual politicians' network was to intimidate reluctant entrepreneurs to pay bribes and, in those areas in which they were well established, to deliver votes. The intimidating atmosphere associated with the Mafia was a further disincentive to any disruption of the corrupt network. The Mafia was assured of high levels of impunity from prosecution by their political contacts. The criminals were also able to share in the profits of businesses with public contracts. A further reciprocal process of benefit was thus set in train by the Mafia involvement in corruption.

The investigations that started the *tangentopoli* scandal began in 1988, but it was in 1992 that the major breakthrough occurred. A socialist politician and manager of a charitable institution in Milan, Mario Chiesa, was arrested receiving a IR£48,000 bribe from the owner of a cleaning company. Chiesa had amassed a large personal fortune (over IR£10 million) despite a modest annual salary (IR£60,000). The information that this seemingly isolated arrest provided snowballed and in just a year a further 130 arrests followed. Many public agencies, for example those with responsibility for roads, environmental services and public transport, were shown to have acted as intermediaries between politicians and businesses. Chiesa's willingness to provide evidence was mirrored by many others. Eventually, even the seven-time Prime Minister Giulio Andreotti was arrested. His network was alleged to have included elements of the Mafia.

The vicious circles involving politicians, administrators, business people and organised crime reinforce each other.

> [They] weaken the market, the state and civil society. Organised crime strengthens corrupt politicians with its bundles of votes and resources of violence, and in turn,

corrupt politicians use their power to enhance the power of the organised crime families supporting them.[25]

The Italian electoral system was easily manipulated. It was designed to prevent one-party majorities, encouraging coalitions and safeguarding small parties' participation in government. The system was altered following a referendum held in the wake of *tangentopoli* revelations in 1993 and the new electoral system reduced the clientelistic potential of smaller parties. The 1994 general election brought new parties and an absolute majority for *Forza Italia*, a newly formed party. Italian politics still feature corruption but at a lower level and in the context of constitutional, administrative and political reforms aimed to control it more effectively.

To draw further lessons for Ireland from the Italian experience, it is worth examining the impact of the economic imperatives of EU membership. Italian governments had struggled to bring the public finances under control. In common with other countries, Italy was very short of the convergence criteria set by the Maastricht Treaty for further European monetary integration. To meet the EU standards and keep Italy in Europe's elite of members, the government was forced to make radical spending cuts. These were even more imperative following the lira's exit from the EMS in September 1992. The result was severe pressure on the clientelist system. Public works contracts, inflated by the needs of politicians' networks, could not be sustained. Public opinion began to favour a more decisive policy of economic management, less state subsidy to industry and more vigorous competitive tendering practices for public works. Each of these, backed by EU pressure, challenged political corruption in Italy. It could be claimed that the Maastricht Agreements put in motion a kind of 'virtuous circle'.[26]

Following the demise of the threat of East European communism, symbolised by the fall of the Berlin Wall in 1989, there was a realignment of political parties. In the new context both the major parties, Christian Democrat and Communist, lost some of their raison d'être. Many of the new parties were outside the clientelist system but gaining electoral support. This outside status of the new political parties destabilised the clientelist networks fundamentally because partisan affiliation had become the litmus test of reliability within the covert, but extensively corrupt, nexus. Corrupt public officials received the support of the established political parties in a mutually profitable and career-enhancing modus operandi that ensured that corruption permeated both state and state-owned institutions. The benefits of corruption, as opposed to honesty, ensured that the numbers involved, and therefore the costs to the taxpayers, increased. This process seriously compromised the invisibility of corruption, the ability of firms to finance it and the profitability of illicit transactions. Politicians' networks had become distinctly unstable by 1992 when a disgruntled small businessperson implicated Chiesa in corrupt dealings.

In the Italian media's reporting of *tangentopoli*, the magistrates were portrayed as heroes in a battle between good and evil.[27] It is important, therefore, to discuss briefly those features of the Italian judicial system that contributed to their significant role. As with the electoral system, the main features of the judicial system reflect the post-war reaction to fascism. The powers of the parliament, central ministry and judicial hierarchy were significantly reduced. Magistrates gained their posts through open competition and enjoyed considerable autonomy. Though there was a degree of continuity of personnel after the war, gradually the social character of the judiciary changed and it became more representative and radical. Both politicians and the Mafia cultivated judges and prosecutors, especially in Rome. Those convicted in provincial courts were often set free in higher courts. Eventually, however, anti-corruption magistrates who pursued a radical and independent agenda secured some key appointments. Their assault on corruption was helped by the change in 1989 to a more adversarial court system, which replaced the former Napoleonic one with judges in the role of interrogators. The new format allowed public prosecutors, part of the same professional cadre as magistrates, to adopt a more co-ordinated strategy towards corruption. Despite its obvious dangers for them, the *mani pulite* investigations were beyond the reach of politicians and, partially by skilful use of the media, enjoyed increasing public support.

The lessons for Ireland of the Italian experience highlight the self-sustaining logic of corruption in the context of constrained political competition, poor standards of public administration and criminal involvement. It is important to note, however, that there are significant differences of scale and intensity between Ireland and Italy. Further, to date, no evidence of Mafia-style involvement has been exposed in the Republic. The question of what type of corruption Ireland is experiencing is important. A sustainable strategy for controlling it depends on properly understanding the problem. To make a judgement on the Irish case, Chapter Two chronicles some of the most relevant instances of corruption.

2. Chronicling Corruption in Irish Politics

It is impossible to know definitively whether or not politically corrupt behaviour is increasing. Any apparent increase may be due to a greater inclination by the media to expose political misdeeds or to more efficient detection by state agencies and others. The recent evidence from Italy and elsewhere, however, suggests that corruption in many countries is rife, widespread and longstanding. It also implies that corruption is not, as was once assumed, 'an aberrant deviation from the norm'[1] when it occurs in established western democracies. 'By the mid 1990s, it appeared that no nation was immune to the corrosive impact of political corruption.'[2]

On the emergence of the issue of political corruption, Garret FitzGerald commented:

> It is especially disturbing that the coincidence of these inquiries . . . has created an impression in the public mind that corruption of one kind or another is a common feature of Irish politics. For this is simply not true. I have from time to time checked with political observers, historians and politicians my belief that no more than about 1 per cent of our national politicians of the past forty years have ever even been suspected of corruption – let alone shown to be corrupt. There are very few countries indeed that could boast as good a record . . . What can, perhaps, be legitimately said is that as the decades have passed this problem seems to have grown from nothing to something.[3]

As FitzGerald suggests, there have been occasional contro-versies about alleged corruption since 1922. These would include the resignation of a minister of state, Dr Con Ward and the Locke's Distillery scandal. On current evidence, however, previous incidents do not compare to the events that have come to light since the early 1990s. There has been a distinct increase in both major and minor examples of political corruption disclosed in the last decade. This chapter reviews:

- early cases of corruption;
- the Beef, McCracken, Moriarty and Flood Tribunals and DIRT Inquiry; and,
- other illustrative incidents.

Early cases of corruption

As suggested above, the paucity of cases before recent decades may be a product of lower levels of exposure. Recent revelations about the Tuskar Rock air tragedy over thirty-two years ago show that too often in the past unpleasant truths were successfully hidden by official and political obstruction and complacency. The original 1970 report into the tragedy failed to deal with some crit-ical issues, details of the plane's maintenance record were absent from the crash investigation report and nothing was said about Aer Lingus's maintenance failures. In July 2000, two international inspectors were appointed to examine the tragedy again.

The Ward Case

Dr Francis Conor Ward was first elected to the Dáil for Monaghan in 1927. He was Parliamentary Secretary for Local Government and Public Health for fourteen years, from 1932. Ward owned a bacon factory at which a manager was dismissed in 1946. A brother of the manager sent a list of allegations against Ward to the Taoiseach, Eamon de Valera, who immediately set up a tribunal of inquiry. It reported within a month. Ward was cleared of all the corruption allegations save one. He had not paid tax on some payments he received from the bacon factory. Ward resigned a week after publication of the tribunal's findings and did not stand at the next general election.

The Locke's Distillery Scandal

The Locke's Distillery scandal of 1947 also led to a tribunal of inquiry. Locke's Distillery had existed since 1757 in Kilbeggan, Co. Westmeath. In 1947 it was for sale. A foreign consortium got the support of the Department of Industry and Commerce to buy the distillery. They were entertained to tea by President Seán T. O'Kelly at Áras an Uachtaráin. Their names were mentioned in the newspapers on 26 September 1947, the day after tea with the President. This publicity led to their exposure as charlatans. One was a Russian using a false British passport. Another had already come to Garda attention and had been told to leave the state. The consortium had worked under the company name of Trans-World. The auctioneer who had acted for Trans-World was a Fianna Fáil senator. He was also a family friend of Seán T. O'Kelly. The Dáil ordered a tribunal of inquiry. The report of the tribunal rejected the allegations made about political collaboration in Trans-World's scheme. A minor official was criticised for a 'grave indiscretion' for allowing the bogus businessmen to compromise the President.

The Beef, McCracken, Moriarty and Flood Tribunals and DIRT Inquiry

In the early 1980s, a series of scandals enveloped the Fianna Fáil Government led by Charles Haughey. Most of these involved abuses of power such as unwarranted telephone tapping and interference with police administration. Nevertheless, they seemed confined to a small group within the Fianna Fáil party. The more recent scandals investigated by the Beef, McCracken, Moriarty and Flood Tribunals and the Dáil revolve around the

TABLE 2.1: The Beef, McCracken, Moriarty and Flood Tribunals and DIRT Inquiry

Instance	Issue	Outcome	Comment
Beef Tribunal (1994)	Govt. mishandles export pro-cedures	Criminal charges, destabilised government	Followed UK media story
Lowry (1996)	Public duties private interests	Resignation and inquiry	Followed media investigation
Haughey (1996)	Unethical receipt of money	Inquiry	Followed media investigation
Burke (1997)	Unethical receipt of money	Resignation and inquiry	Followed media investigation
AIB: Bogus Ac-counts (1998)	Evasion of DIRT	PAC inquiry	Followed media investigation
Flynn (1998)	Claims of receipt of IR£50,000	Not re-appointed to EU, investiga-tion by inquiry	Followed media investigation
Redmond (1999)	Unethical receipt of money	Tax investigation by CAB, investi-gation by inquiry	Followed reve-lations at Flood Tribunal
Ellis (1999)	Receipt of money from CJ Haughey from Party Leader's Account, NIB writing off of debt	Resignation as chairman of Oir-eachtas Committee, debate on treat-ment of debts of politicians by banks	From Moriarty Tribunal
Foley (2000)	Ansbacher account holder	Resignation as vice-chairman and member of PAC, 30-day suspension from Dáil	From Moriarty Tribunal

issue of politicians, money and relationships with business, see Table 2.1.

The Beef Tribunal

In August 1994, a report from a Tribunal of Inquiry was issued concerning the Irish beef-processing industry. The industry, which accounted for 34 per cent of the Republic's agricultural output, was by 1991 dominated by Goodman International and its associated companies. However, Larry Goodman, the owner, had suffered several major business setbacks and was in deep financial trouble in 1991. The Report of the Beef Tribunal was called for by the Dáil following allegations in a British television *World in Action* documentary broadcast in May 1991 about irregularities in the administration of export credit guarantees. These guarantees protect firms from losses resulting from non-payment of monies owed to Irish exporters by foreign firms. In addition to the Tribunal's findings, a subsequent court case found that serious crimes were committed at one of the Goodman meat plants. The court sentenced two Goodman executives to suspended prison terms for their parts in a conspiracy to defraud the Minister for Agriculture by misappropriating intervention beef. The two executives neither instigated nor benefited from the fraud. The unidentified authors of the scheme were not prosecuted.

Serious charges were made in the Dáil before the setting up of the Tribunal. Established parliamentary methods, however, were unable to elicit the full facts. Many of the allegations made by TDs involved criminal activity. The central political figure was the then Taoiseach Albert Reynolds. Following the Report of the Tribunal, Reynolds assumed all responsibility for decisions made on the allocation of export credit guarantees on consignments of beef for Iraq by which Goodman benefited immensely while he was Minister for Industry and Commerce in 1987 and 1988. The Tribunal found that Reynolds was legally entitled to make the decisions he did and that he had acted in good faith. There was no suggestion of personal financial gain by any politician involved. Nevertheless, the Beef Tribunal does highlight some areas of concern about the way politicians and private companies relate to each other. These included:

1. the role of personal friendships;
2. the probity and reasonableness of government procedures; and,
3. political party funding.

It is hard to distinguish between close relationships, which may develop between successful business leaders and senior politicians, and personal friendships. For Charles Haughey, his own lifestyle probably made it inevitable that his friends would be drawn from the business elite. Haughey was known to have been friendly with people like Larry Goodman, Dermot Desmond, Michael Smurfit and Bernie Cahill, who was not only the chairman of the Board of Greencore but also of Aer Lingus and Feltrim, a mining company largely owned by Charles's son, Conor. These people were part of what was being called the 'golden circle' – a group of top businessmen for whom the Government seemed particularly facilitatory.[4]

The promise of massive investment in a major Irish industry may have contributed to politicians making poor judgements in an effort to support Goodman's business, but they were motivated, according to the Tribunal, by their interpretation of the national interest rather than possible personal gain.

The Report of the Beef Tribunal did not allocate blame to anyone for the staggering irregularities which it uncovered in the way employees of Goodman International conducted their business.[5] Nor did it seek to pin responsibility for the inadequate control exercised by government departments. The proceedings of the inquiry, however, were characterised by seemingly daily revelations of malpractice and systematic fraud in the handling of beef exports, by bitter personal accusations made by the most senior of political figures about each other, and by a depressing catalogue of incompetence in the management of public affairs. As a result, it did seriously damage the standing of the political process and raised disturbing questions about the quality of public administration in the Republic.

The Beef Tribunal brought to prominence the financial links between businesses and political organisations. Private companies in the Republic are free to give money to politicians and political parties. It was suggested that Goodman had been given special treatment because of contributions he had made to Fianna Fáil. The record of his companies on investment, job creation and increased market share had been spectacular. The basis of this success had been exporting Irish beef to new markets. The Report accepted that Goodman had not been shown favouritism by Fianna Fáil alone and, importantly, that the Fine Gael/Labour coalition government had been just as helpful to him.

Private companies, it emerged, make donations to all of the major parties without expecting particular benefits. There is, however, an easy assumption shared by the political and business elite that what is good for Irish companies generally, especially those in the export field, is beneficial to the Republic as a whole. This outlook is thought to be particularly prevalent in Fianna Fáil, the party that has dominated government since the 1930s and pioneered Ireland's development strategy in the late 1950s and 1960s. The issue of funding political parties has become a central issue through the more recent Moriarty and Flood Tribunals.

McCracken Tribunal

Revelations in the *Irish Independent* in November 1996 about disclosures made during a court battle between members of the family who owned the major retail chain, Dunnes Stores, initiated the events which were to lead to the establishment of the McCracken Tribunal. A Fine Gael cabinet member, Michael Lowry, was accused of failing to disclose payments from Ben Dunne, one of the family members. Ministers are obliged to make a declaration of their tax affairs to the Taoiseach on appointment. Lowry did not make a full disclosure. He did not tell the Taoiseach that he had availed of the 1993 tax amnesty. He also had IR£395,107 spent on his home in Tipperary paid for by Dunnes Stores under a deal involving his own refrigeration firm. He eventually resigned from office despite initially refusing to go. In December, it was reported that a prominent Fianna Fáil politician (later revealed to be Charles Haughey) had also received more than IR£1 million from Ben Dunne.

Throughout 1997, a further series of revelations by the press kept the question of payments to individual politicians and to political parties to the forefront of public attention. An official inquiry, the McCracken Tribunal, established that there was no evidence that Lowry had received money through Dunne in return for political favours. He had, however, left himself vulnerable to pressure from Dunnes Stores. The Tribunal exposed a web of offshore accounts and convoluted transactions designed to avoid tax. Most spectacularly, the inquiry began to shed light on the sources of Haughey's wealth. Very large sums of money were channelled to the former Taoiseach from the so-called 'Ansbacher accounts'. Haughey was forced to admit receiving IR£1.3 million from Ben Dunne.[6] So complex and secret were the Ansbacher accounts that a further tribunal under High Court Judge Michael Moriarty was set up to investigate all payments to politicians.

Moriarty Tribunal

The Moriarty Tribunal was established by Dáil Éireann in September 1997.[7] It is centrally investigating payments to Haughey and Lowry and whether any political decision might have been made by either when in office which might have benefited a 'person or company' who made a payment.

Haughey's income had been a cause for much speculation. It became evident that not all the money being received by Haughey was from Dunne. A number of major revelations with regard to money received and spent by Haughey have emerged to date. The Tribunal uncovered the writing off by AIB of nearly IR£400,000 in debts, the spending of the party leader's fund on expensive Charvet shirts, exclusive restaurants and paying a debt to avoid bankruptcy for a Fianna Fáil back-bencher, John Ellis. It also disclosed the depositing of funds collected for medical bills in the United States for the late Brian Lenihan TD in the party leader's account and allegations that Haughey retained election donations to Fianna Fáil for his personal use.

To date, the Tribunal has suggested that Haughey was funded from private sources to the tune of IR£8.5 million and that he evaded paying tax on these gifts. In April 2000, he settled with the Revenue Commissioners for just over a million pounds in tax on the gift of IR£1.3 million from Dunne. This was verified in the report of the McCracken Tribunal. The sale of Carysfort College in 1990 is also being investigated by the Tribunal.

The McCracken Tribunal confirmed that money was held on deposit in certain Irish banks by offshore banks for the benefit of Irish residents including Haughey. These deposits became known as the 'Ansbacher accounts' after the name of the bank in the Cayman Islands. The Ansbacher accounts revealed millions of pounds which clearly were not all destined for Haughey. The report of the authorised officer from the Department of Enterprise, Trade and Employment was given to the Moriarty and Flood Tribunals and to the Revenue Commissioners. A retired President of the High Court, Declan Costello, is carrying out an inquiry into the Ansbacher deposits.

Flood Tribunal

Local government decision-making on land use planning has been an area of suspicion for some years. Particularly in the Dublin environs, the rezoning of land to make it available for housing or industrial use very greatly increases its value. In 1995, Colm Mac Eochaidh, a barrister, and Michael Smith, the current chair of An Taisce, advertised in *The Irish Times,* anonymously offering a reward of IR£10,000 for information on land rezoning corruption that would lead to a conviction. Information was to be sent to a firm of Newry-based solicitors. Among those who gave information was James Gogarty, who was central to the resignation of Ray Burke and the establishment of the Flood Tribunal.

The Flood Tribunal was established in October 1997[8] to investigate the persistent and disturbing allegations of political corruption in the planning process. A retired building company executive, James Gogarty, was a key figure in the setting up of the tribunal. Gogarty claimed that former Minister, Ray Burke, received donations to the value of IR£80,000 although Burke acknowledges that he only received IR£30,000. Burke testified to the Tribunal that he operated an offshore account based in Jersey between 1984 and 1993. In a three-week period in May 1989, the then Minister for Justice and Communications lodged IR£107,100 into the bank. He received IR£35,000 in May 1989 from the chief executive, deputy chairman, and a director of Century Radio, Oliver Barry, who was also a concert promoter. The Independent Radio and Television Commission awarded the first national independent radio licence to Century. Burke, as the Minister responsible for broadcasting policy, had no role in the allocation of licences. A delay in the start-up of the new station was caused by an argument with RTÉ, the national broadcasting network, over its transmission fees. RTÉ was demanding an annual fee of IR£614,000 for broadcasting Century's signal on RTÉ's nationwide transmission network. In March 1989, Burke forced RTÉ to drop its price, effectively saving Century over IR£500,000.

In June 1989, Burke received IR£30,000 from James Gogarty on behalf of Joseph Murphy Structural Engineering (JMSE) and a further IR£30,000 from Rennick's Manufacturing, a subsidiary of Fitzwilton, the holding company controlled by Dr Tony O'Reilly and his family. Dr O'Reilly is one of Ireland's most prominent international businessmen with worldwide interests in the media and food production. The disclosures of the JMSE donation precipitated Burke's resignation as a minister and deputy in September 1997.

Another central figure at the Flood Tribunal has been the former Dublin assistant city and county manager, George

Redmond. Gogarty gave evidence that Redmond received a payment of IR£15,000 from the Murphy Group in 1989, in relation to the impending expiration of planning permission on land in north Dublin. Redmond insisted that he was never involved in corruption but had a number of developers and clients to whom he gave 'advice' in return for a fee.[9] Redmond was found guilty of tax offences and has made a settlement with the Revenue Commissioners for over IR£750,000. He was also fined IR£7,500 on pleading guilty to ten charges of tax evasion but was not given a jail sentence. He denied to the Flood Tribunal that he received money for planning favours. However, he did admit to receiving IR£25,000 'hello money' for introducing Gogarty to Michael Bailey of Bovale Developments. Redmond also received IR£10,000 from the former chairman of National Toll Roads, Tom Roche Snr, who said that Redmond had been 'extremely helpful' in relation to land acquisition for the IR£31 million motorway scheme. Redmond's only known source of income was his salary as assistant city and county manager, yet he had amassed a fortune of over one million pounds. By 1998, he had assets worth IR£1,051,360 even though he never earned a salary of more than IR£29,000 a year. In the 1960s his savings were running at twice his income for the decade; by the 1970s, they were five times his earnings. The Tribunal continues to investigate the sources of his wealth. Redmond is the most senior official to be implicated in corrupt practices. The payments for 'advice' were from developers interested in planning decisions.

The Flood Tribunal is also investigating another allegation concerning a former Minister for the Environment. In June 1989, the Minister, Padraig Flynn, received a donation of IR£50,000, which its donor, London-based property developer Tom Gilmartin, has stated was intended for the Fianna Fáil Party. Flynn was one of the two Fianna Fáil National Treasurers. He, however, insists that the monies were for his own personal campaign. It is expected that Flynn will be called before the Tribunal. Arising from publicity surrounding this issue Flynn was not reappointed as Ireland's EU Commissioner in 2000. Gilmartin has suggested that when he comes before the Tribunal his evidence will bring down the government. As well as the 'Flynn donation', he makes allegations about development projects including Quarryvale.

In April 2000, a public affairs lobbyist, Frank Dunlop, made his first appearances at the Flood Tribunal. Dunlop is a former Government press secretary with very strong Fianna Fáil connections. He has alleged that he 'bribed' councillors for their votes for rezonings of Quarryvale and other major developments in County Dublin in the 1990s. The councillors claim what they received were political and election donations. Further details are anticipated on the investigations by the Tribunal. The Dunlop revelations prompted Fianna Fáil and Fine Gael to carry out their own internal inquiries.[10] The Fianna Fáil inquiry has led to the resignation of Liam Lawlor TD from the party. Three Fine Gael councillors are in dispute over the findings of their party's inquiry that has raised questions over some of their donation details. Both inquiries found that the vast majority of contributions were legitimate election donations. However, media speculation is that councillors did not disclose full details to these internal inquiries and that the tribunal, which has extensive powers of discovery, particularly in relation to bank accounts, will lead to further revelations.

DIRT Inquiry

Deposit interest retention tax (DIRT) was introduced for interest paid by banks or building societies by the Finance Act, 1986 and is still collected. In April 1998, reports in the press highlighted the use of 'bogus' non-resident accounts as a means of evading DIRT by Allied Irish Bank (AIB). This prompted the Public Accounts Committee (PAC) to investigate the matter. In October 1998, the PAC inquiry was extended to cover other financial institutions and the Revenue Commissioners. PAC asked about the information known to the financial institutions and regulatory authorities concerning the use of bogus non-resident accounts. Following new legislation,[11] the Comptroller and

Auditor General (C & AG) uncovered widespread use of bogus non-resident accounts. The Report of the C & AG formed the book of evidence for the inquiry carried out by the PAC.

The DIRT Inquiry revealed that up to 300,000 bogus non-resident accounts were used around the state by customers of all the major banks to dodge DIRT and other taxes during the 1980s and early 1990s. Bank branch managers aided tax evaders as a means of attracting business. It emerged that senior figures in the financial industries, the Revenue Commissioners and the Department of Finance were aware of this practice but never tackled the issue. Significantly, the Finance Act, 1986 that empowered the Revenue Commissioners to inspect non-residence declarations held by the financial institutions, was not allowed to be invoked by revenue inspectors.

The PAC Report was published in December 1999.[12] In response, the Bank of Ireland, in July 2000, paid IR£30.5 million to the Revenue Commissioners in settlement of its DIRT liability. It is anticipated the other banks will also make settlements with the Revenue. The DIRT Inquiry reflected the effectiveness and efficiency of using a parliamentary inquiry as a method of investigation.

In addition, as the bogus non-resident accounts represented wholesale criminality within the small business and professional classes, facilitated by the banks, so was the Ansbacher scheme the 'elite' mechanism of tax evasion. Tax evasion was recognised as a serious issue by the government as far back as January 1988 when it introduced its first tax amnesty. At that time, IR£500 million was received by the Revenue Commissioners without interest or penalties demanded. This was followed by the 1993 tax amnesty, which netted about IR£200 million.

As discussed earlier, Ansbacher Cayman was used to hold vast resources offshore for many of Ireland's wealthiest people. Des Traynor, a leading accountant and Haughey's own personal accountant, managed the deposits. The money was held by Ansbacher Cayman earning interest for the depositors. Traynor opened a 'mirror' account in Guinness and Mahon private bank which allowed his clients to have access to the money although it remained technically 'offshore' and untaxable. The McCracken Tribunal established that in 1989 there was IR£38 million in the accounts, two of which were for the benefit of Haughey. All the accounts had secret codes to ensure privacy and security. Investigations on behalf of the Minister for Enterprise, Trade and Employment produced a report in September 1999 that estimated that the Ansbacher operation serviced 120 of Ireland's wealthiest people. Many regard the scheme as tax evasion for a 'golden circle' of elite professionals and business people. Whilst the details of the account holders have not been published some names have come into the public domain. A further list of approximately 40 people emerged when the Moriarty Tribunal disclosed that Denis Foley TD was an account holder. He was not on the first list of 120.

The Foley Affair (2000)

The Fianna Fáil TD for Kerry North, Denis Foley, was revealed as an Ansbacher account holder following the Moriarty Tribunal revelations and he subsequently resigned as vice-chairman of the Public Accounts Committee (PAC). The Dáil Committee on Members' Interests investigated whether the TD had breached the Ethics in Public Office Act, 1995. Foley had voted in the Dáil in September 1997 against broadening the terms of reference of the Moriarty Tribunal to include looking at the Ansbacher accounts and had not declared that he had a material interest in the subject matter. As a result, the Dáil suspended him for thirty days.

The Ellis Affair (1999)

The 'Ellis Affair' emerged from the Moriarty Tribunal and its investigations into the use of the Fianna Fáil leader's account. In late 1989, the Fianna Fáil TD, John Ellis, was facing financial and political ruin. The cattle-dealing and meat-processing business he had built with his brother in the 1970s had collapsed and creditors, who were owed nearly IR£300,000, had issued bankruptcy proceedings. National Irish Bank was owed IR£263,450;

two marts were owed IR£13,600 and IR£12,400 respectively. In addition, several Roscommon farmers had taken their case to the High Court seeking IR£30,000. Ellis could not pay the debts but a declaration of bankruptcy would result in the loss of his Dáil seat. Ellis' main creditor, National Irish Bank accepted IR£20,000 in full settlement of the debt and wrote off IR£240,000.

At this time, December 1989, the Fianna Fáil/Progressive Democrat coalition had the smallest of Dáil majorities and Haughey did not want to face a by-election. He gave Ellis IR£12,400 in cash, which he took from the Fianna Fáil party leader's account, to pay one of the marts. In March 1990, Haughey gave Ellis a further IR£13,600 from the same account, to pay the second mart debt.

Other Illustrative Incidents

While the Tribunals have provided a focus to the major cases other incidents are also important in illustrating the pattern of corruption in the Republic, see Table 2.2.

Irish Sugar Company (1991)

The privatisation of the Irish Sugar Company provided one of the first major controversies of the 1990s. This once loss-making, state-owned enterprise had become profitable under the tough management of Chris Comerford. He was allegedly involved in a company which had been lent money by Irish Sugar in order to buy 49 per cent of another company in which Irish Sugar was the major shareholder (51 per cent). This minority shareholding was later sold to the parent company at what was widely regarded as an inflated price and one that could not be sustained on the basis of the subsidiary's performance. A group of managers, including Comerford, realised a profit of IR£7m in what was perceived to be a risk-free transaction. The scandal in this case was seen to arise from possible conflicts of interest between the public duties and private interests of the chief executive of a state-owned company.

TABLE 2.2: Other Illustrative Incidents

Instance	Issue	Outcome	Comment
Irish Sugar Co (1991)	Public duties and private interests-	Resignation of chief executive	Increased awareness of public sector behaviour
Telecom Éireann (1991)	Public duties and private interests	Resignation of chair of the board	Increased reluctance of business elite to serve
Celtic Helicopters (1991)	Insider information	Weakened government reputation	Reinforced public disquiet
C & D Petfoods (1994)	Public duties and private interests	No resignation	Taoiseach's judgement questioned
Coveney (1995)	Public duties and private interests	Demotion	Followed Irish media story
Celtic Helicopters (1998)	Investment by individuals requested by CJ Haughey	Department inquiry	McCracken and Moriarty Tribunals
Political Parties (1998)	Pick-me-ups	Revenue Commissioners-Investigation	Followed media investigation
Sheedy Affair (1998)	Unorthodox early release of prisoner	Inquiry by Chief Justice, resignations of judges and officials	Media and Parliamentry questions
FitzGerald (1999)	AIB writing off of debt	Privilege for politician	Followed media investigation
Duffy (1999)	Public duties and private interests	Resignation as special advisor to the Taoiseach	Followed media investigation
Harney and McCreevy (1999)	Acceptance of free holiday at French villa	No breach of Cabinet guidelines, public disquiet	Followed media investigation
Woodchester (1999)	Write off of election debt to four senior Labour figures	Public focus on treatment by banks of political personalities	Followed media investigation
O'Flaherty (2000)	Government-nominee after resignation from Supreme Court re Sheedy affair	Massive public disquiet, defeat for Government in by-election, loss of support for coalition	Arose from Government nomination as vice-president of European Investment Bank

For a fuller account see Collins, *Political Issues in Ireland Today* (Manchester UP, 1999)

Telecom Éireann (1991)

Another state-owned enterprise, Telecom Éireann, was at the centre of a row in 1991. The company board paid IR£9.4m for a property for its new headquarters despite a valuation of IR£6m by the State Valuation Office. The allegations of impropriety arose from the fact that the government-appointed chairman of Telecom, Michael Smurfit, had links with United Property Holdings, the company selling the property. An official report into the affair found that, while the chairman did have a shareholding in the company concerned, he had not exercised any undue influence in Telecom's purchase of the property. This matter created serious concern at the time. The allegations of corruption appeared to gain currency when the Taoiseach requested the chairman to 'stand aside' pending investigations.

Celtic Helicopters (1991)

The names of several leading businessmen were thrust into the public domain by the Irish Sugar and Telecom affairs. In particular Dermot Desmond, a stockbroker was further implicated in another. This centred on information of a sensitive commercial nature about the helicopter subsidiary of the airline Aer Lingus, for which Desmond's company was acting as an advisor. The information came into the possession of a rival company, Celtic Helicopters, which was owned by the son of the Taoiseach, Charles Haughey. The incident became public when it was discovered that Desmond had sent the information that he was apparently intending to give to Celtic Helicopters to Aer Lingus instead, through a 'postal error'.

The Irish Sugar, Telecom Éireann and Celtic Helicopters incidents each contributed to public unease, not just with business people but with politicians as well. This was reflected in a public opinion poll in December 1991; in an *Irish Times* survey, 65 per cent of respondents thought 'corruption was a widespread and serious problem amongst our elected politicians'.

Pick-me-ups: Political Parties (1998)

Pick-me-ups is the term applied to one type of financial relationship, exposed in 1998, between political parties and their wealthy backers. Companies paid debts for the party, for example a printing bill, transport costs or catering facilities at a conference. There were advantages for the donors contributing to political parties in this manner, rather than election donations. The payments could be hidden from auditors and shareholders, passed off as legitimate business expenses and could subsequently be written off against corporation tax. The company might even claim back VAT on the payment. When this practice was exposed, it emerged it had been used by all the main parties. The Revenue Commissioners carried out an investigation.

Preferential treatment by financial institutions

It is accepted that banks write off bad debts but the disclosures that a number of financial institutions were involved in clearing very large and small debts for a number of politicians gave a public perception of two laws, one for the ordinary citizen, another for the powerful. Two former Taoisigh, Haughey and FitzGerald, had substantial loans written off by Allied Irish Bank. As mentioned earlier, Ellis had over IR£240,000 of debt cancelled by National Irish Bank. A loan to fund the unsuccessful European election campaign of Labour Party candidate, Orla Guerin, was written off by Woodchester Bank in 1996. Dick Spring, Labour Party Leader (1982–1997), guaranteed this loan with three other individuals. The bank made a political donation to offset the debt of IR£28,000. Smaller amounts were cancelled for one or two other deputies. Speculation exists that more politicians have benefited from the 'benevolence' of financial institutions than is publicly known.

Passports

The passport for investment scheme was designed to promote employment investment in Irish companies but was abolished in 1998 amid a controversy that it was a route for wealthy non-nationals to purchase Irish passports. When the scheme was discontinued, 163 people had received passports and IR£95 million had been invested in Irish firms.

Two cases were particularly controversial. Sheikh Mahfouz, a wealthy Arab businessman, paid an estimated IR£20 million for eleven passports, which were processed in 1990 by the Minister for Justice, Ray Burke. The granting of these passports is expected to be part of the Flood Tribunal due to the involvement of Burke. They may also come under consideration at the Moriarty Tribunal because of the role of the Taoiseach Charles Haughey, at whose home the passports were delivered to Sheikh Mahfouz.

The granting of passports to the Masri family from Palestine in 1992 became an issue of much debate and the subject of an internal government inquiry in 1994 when Albert Reynolds was Taoiseach. C & D Foods, a company that was established by Albert Reynolds and owned by his family, got IR£1.1 million from the Masri family as a loan on very favourable terms.

The Duffy Affair

In December 1998, Paddy Duffy, special adviser to Taoiseach Bertie Ahern, became a director of public relations and lobbying firm, Dillon Consultants. Dillons were acting for NTL who were buying Cablelink. In April 1999, a perceived conflict of interest was highlighted by a Fine Gael Deputy to the Minister for Public Enterprise who discussed the matter with the Taoiseach. Duffy denied any connection with the company but was forced to resign his special adviser's position in June 1999 on publication of the story by *The Irish Times*. The Public Office Commission decided against a full investigation of the Duffy case but were critical of both the Taoiseach and Duffy. The Commission asked:

> . . . whether or not more needs to be done to ensure that special advisers and, indeed, career civil servants are always conscious of the potential conflicts which may arise where they are exercising functions which impinge on the activities of firms or companies with which they may have working relationships at some future date . . .[13]

The Sheedy Affair

In April 1999, three senior law officers, including both a Supreme and High Court judge, resigned following what became known as the 'Sheedy affair'. This revolved around a controversial court directive that released an architect, Philip Sheedy, from prison. He had served only twelve months of a four-year sentence imposed in 1997 after a road accident in Dublin in which a young mother was killed.

The DPP successfully challenged the decision to release Sheedy on the grounds that 'improper practices' may have been involved. A judicial review overturned the decision and Sheedy voluntarily returned to prison. There had been no suggestion of financial corruption. The Chief Justice carried out an investigation of the case. In his report, the Chief Justice documented how – following representations from a member of Mr Sheedy's family – Supreme Court Judge, Mr Justice Hugh O'Flaherty, had called the County Registrar and asked whether the Sheedy case might be relisted for hearing. The County Registrar contacted Mr Sheedy's legal representative and advised him to apply for a review and set the case in motion. The hearing came before High Court Judge, Mr Justice Cyril Kelly. The Chief Justice found that while Mr O'Flaherty's involvement in the case had arisen from a spirit of humanitarianism, he was responsible for causing the case to be re-listed. His intervention was deemed inappropriate and unwise and was damaging to the administration of justice. An Oireachtas committee rejected a proposal to set up a tribunal.

The O'Flaherty Affair

In May 2000, the Government nominated former Supreme Court Judge, Hugh O'Flaherty, to a IR£147,000-per-annum post as a vice-president of the European Investment Bank. Opinion polls suggested, and the results of a by-election in June indicate, that this appointment utterly aggrieved the public who viewed it as cronyism and 'golden circle' treatment. This action resulted in the most serious setback to the Fianna Fáil/Progressive

Democrat government since it took office in June 1997. Many commentators regard it as the turning point for the government and it may have brought the end of the government closer.

Conclusion

Ireland has experienced dramatic changes over the last twenty-five years. The decline in the influence of the political establishment resulting from corruption has been matched by a weakening in the standing of the Catholic Church, following revelations of sex abuse. Other organisations, such as the financial institutions, have also suffered falling prestige. Tribunals and inquiries surrounding major health scandals have also been taking place. The events chronicled in this chapter must be seen in the context of a broader challenge to the major social and political institutions.

3. The Causes of Corruption

The incidents outlined in Chapter Two provide a basis for understanding the causes of corruption in Ireland. In this chapter, some of the more significant influences found in the literature will be examined:

    a.   historical developments;
    b.   longevity in power;
    c.   increased state activity;
    d.   ethical leadership;
    e.   financing of political parties; and,
    f.   political career patterns.

Historical Developments

The Republic of Ireland has been independent since 1922. Corruption, however, has a longer history. Much contemporary commentary takes a rather short perspective and this has led to a view that Ireland's experience of corruption followed

> . . . the elite generational change that occurred
> between 1957 and 1965, when old revolution-
> aries, often begrudgingly and with great
> foreboding, gave way to younger people.[1]

O'Leary[2] suggests a slightly earlier date when he describes
1951 as 'the first genuine "pork-barrel" election in Ireland'.
Others see the leadership struggle within Fianna Fáil as the
signal of a fundamental change. The main rivals were Charles
Haughey and George Colley.

> Their rivalry was to develop into a life-long enmity . . .
> In 1966, Haughey, with his close connections in the
> business worlds, was seen as the leading representative
> of the men in the mohair suits, whose flamboyant
> lifestyle and social ambitions he so obviously shared.
> Colley was the clean-cut Irish-speaking bearer of an
> older tradition, concerned, he was to say, lest low
> standards in high places damage Irish life.[3]

These 'sea change' accounts, which emphasise a radical turn
of events, are persuasive in many respects. They neglect,
however, the extent to which the civil service and, more
particularly, local government had been in Irish hands for two
decades before 1922. According to Arthur Griffith, a leader of the
struggle for Independence, the Local Government Board was the
'fountainhead of corruption' in Ireland.[4]

> The 1898 Act also had the incidental effect of setting up
> a permanent antagonism between local nationalists
> (and, occasionally, unionists) and the British
> government's Local Government Board, a central co-
> ordinating and grant-aiding body that gave generous
> financial assistance to the local authorities and
> attempted to curb their more extravagant essays in
> local preference and spendthrift schemes . . . Resent-
> ment of and contempt for the perceived corruption of
> local authorities was widespread . . . These attitudes
> animated much of Sinn Féin's drive towards reform,
> centralisation, and standardisation of employment

conditions. In general, the Sinn Féiners wished to clean up what were seen, with some accuracy, as local Tammany Halls as being unworthy of the idealistic visions of either the founders of Sinn Féin or the martyrs of Easter Week.[5]

Further, the sea change approach fails to account for the resolute action that the first Irish regime had to take against local councils across its jurisdiction to counter widespread nepotism, jobbery and dubious financial transactions. Even though Eamon de Valera eased the element of control over local appointments on coming to office in 1932, he soon had to reimpose it.[6] Between 1927 and 1939, state intervention in the economy become more marked with nineteen new state-sponsored companies being formed.[7]

> The economic growth rate for . . . 1922 to 1938 has been estimated at 1.2 percent per year, at 0 percent during the war years and at only 1.8 percent after the war. That rate . . . was considerably slower than other European nations and was supported not by investment in industry but by government spending on social services, agriculture and housing.[8]

Many qualified graduates, especially women, found that the claims of merit in public sector employment were hampered by a lack of 'connections' and, in the harsh labour market of the 1930s and 1940s, were obliged to emigrate.

The early local government corrupt actions are normally blamed on the instability of the revolutionary period and the civil war that followed independence. They show, however, that corruption is not just a recent experience in Ireland while pointing, at the same time, to the relevance of long-term cultural and historical experience. Addressing the issues of clientelism and merit recruitment in the public service, Garvin hints at a similar judgement:

> What is clear . . . is that many Irish people are deeply pessimistic about the possibility of government being

> honest and impersonal . . . [The] pattern of individual-
> istic responses to political problems is far more
> pronounced in Ireland than in other western liberal
> democracies. It was presumably even more
> pronounced forty years ago. What is almost surprising
> is the apparently relative absence of favouritism and
> corruption on a large scale, given the poverty and
> culture of the society.[9]

Similarly, given that Ireland pursued a policy of protectionism, principally following the election of Fianna Fáil in 1932 and
under all governments until the late 1950s, it now seems
unlikely that corruption was not present. National leaders may
have been intolerant of corruption.[10] The system, however,
permitted businesses to seek protective tariffs in cases of 'undue
competition' or 'overproduction'. As Murphy intimates,
'Industrial protection . . . ran the risk of carrying the burden of
inefficient and slothful, if not corrupt, manufacturers'.[11] Just such
arrangements have been the focus of unethical behaviour in
other jurisdictions. Irish research in this area is, however, very
sparse and much empirical research needs to be done.

In the same manner, large-scale infrastructural projects
involving foreign contractors, such as the Ardnacrusha
hydroelectric scheme completed by a German company in 1926,
have been the occasion for corruption or rent seeking in newly-
independent developing nations. Research from such
jurisdictions suggests that nation-building programmes of this
kind can lead to corruption if the use of state power blurs the
distinction between public and private interests. In the Irish case,
however, there is no direct evidence of wrongdoing.

> . . . even Eamon de Valera had the tongues wagging at
> times, despite living in accordance with his own
> doctrine of frugal comfort . . . de Valera exhibited no
> ostentation with property, yachts, helicopters, race
> horses or expensive wines, but back in the 1920s there
> was more than a little controversy about the $5 million
> that he had collected in the United States during 1920.[12]

De Valera, a leader in the struggle for independence, collected money in America in the name of the 'Irish Republic', but when the government of the day tried to get hold of it, they were blocked because they needed de Valera's signature. When the government sued for control of the money, the American courts ruled that it should be returned to those who had given it. De Valera persuaded many of the donors to support the establishment of the *Irish Press* newspaper.

> Years later there was controversy over the way in which
> the de Valera family, in effect, took over the ownership
> of the newspaper to which so many ordinary people,
> both here and in the United States, had contributed.[13]

De Valera was further embarrassed by revelations in 1958 that he owned substantial shares in the *Irish Press* despite his statement that he held only 'fiduciary interest'.[14]

At its foundation, the legitimacy of the Irish state was significantly contested and its economic resources were low. The ruling elite struggled to establish a new police force, to assert the primacy of civilian control of the military and, as was noted above, to ensure probity in the bureaucracy.[15] The modern comparative literature suggests that, in this stage of political development, the distinction between state and private interests may be masked by a regime's claim to speak for 'the people'. Interestingly, Robinson suggests that these dangers were less pronounced in former British colonies than their Francophone counterparts because of: '. . . a tradition of press freedom, durable legal institutions, an emphasis on elite education and British civil service norms of probity and impartiality'.[16]

These factors were indeed present in Ireland. The ready identification of state and private interest is, however, a feature of some of the cases cited above, notably in the case of the Beef Tribunal. It is clear that ministers and, to some extent, civil servants viewed the success of certain beef enterprises as in the wider national interest.

Even with the abandonment of protectionism in the 1960s, Ireland's model of development depended on a high level of state involvement. This level of engagement could not survive the fiscal crisis, inflation and rise of the foreign debt in the 1970s. The state's relations with business became more ambiguous and facilitatory.[17] It is possible that the Republic's encouragement of foreign investment through a favourable tax regime and other incentives led to a more cavalier attitude among Irish business people. This approach was further reinforced by the failings of company law and accountancy practice.

Longevity in power

> Another potential cause of political corruption which merits attention is longevity in power, or at least the feeling that political power is not threatened by realistic challengers or alternatives.[18]

A political party that has been in power for long periods even, as with the Italian Christian Democrats in coalition, may come to see its fortunes as interwoven with those of the institutions of government. Others may also be encouraged to do so.

> In a democratic system, political competition . . . .should . . . help deter 'bad behaviour' by politicians in power limiting the willingness of public agents to indulge in illegal activity. The competition between different parties and individuals aspiring to govern should help those who are most honest or more willing to denounce the illegal actions of others . . . The dynamics of the Italian political system, however, have powerfully limited this possibility.[19]

Most analysts would categorise the Italian case as systemic corruption. Nevertheless, as discussed in Chapter One, the Italian example has some resonance for Ireland. In this case:

> [o]n the government side, the absence of turnover weakened the capacity of planning, favouring instead

the immediate interest in dividing up and occupying public offices for clientelistic ends . . . . In the management of the public and semi-public agencies and in the enterprises with public capital, members of those very parties that had nominated their protégés inside the administrative bodies were in charge of the institutional controls.[20]

In Ireland, the ascendancy of Fianna Fáil since the 1930s was effectively ended in 1989 when it accepted the role of competitive party and coalition partner rather than a national movement. Nevertheless, the party has been in power for eight of the subsequent eleven years.

Appointees to state-sponsored companies have been at the centre of a number of the incidents outlined above. Some idea of the scale of government patronage can be gauged from the more than 1,159 appointments made to the boards of state agencies by the Fianna Fáil–Progressive Democrat government in its first thirty months. It assumed office in 1997.

[These] appointments to State boards, covering all areas of Government activity. The appointees include professional experts and those rewarded for political support . . . [M]any board members receive a fixed annual payment ranging from IR£2,000 to over IR£7,000 along with expenses.[21]

Even when membership of such a board may not be particularly remunerative, it can afford significant advantages in business intelligence, networking and social cachet. For some, they clearly also provided rent-seeking opportunities. Opportunities to make appointments are a valuable political asset for ministers. The level of discretion may, however, be exaggerated as professional expertise or the expectations of the social partners influence many nominations. The longer a party holds office the greater will be the extent of its patronage.

Increased State Activity

In common with other European countries, Ireland has seen a major expansion in the scale, scope and size of state activity. Some of the funding has been from the EU but the money is administered at state and local levels. Senior officials at the Department of Finance '. . . recognises the problem posed where the political and farming pressure is to get out payments speedily as against the necessary need to have proper controls in place'.[22]

The trend in state activity has led to an expanded bureaucracy with increased discretionary powers, much of it exercised at local level through municipalities, health boards and the decentralised offices of government departments. Della Porta identifies these two factors as promoting the development of corruption:

> . . . the increased number of decisions taken in the public rather than the private sector, and administrative decentralisation [. . .] increases the number of decision-making centres. The growth of welfare programmes, the expansion of the public sector and the proliferation of laws and regulations all favour the spread of corruption. Moreover, local government opens a much broader potential field to corruption because of the large number of private contracts that are made and the likelihood of avoiding scrutiny by the central government.[23]

Many of the cases of fraud or embezzlement involving public servants arise from subsidy regimes in agriculture, licensing of vehicles, tax administration and the like. Speaking to the Dáil Public Accounts Committee on 6 July 1999, an official of the Department of Agriculture admitted that '. . . there is fraud and no-one can dispute that. [But] only a couple of hundred cases are involved'. From the criminal trial that followed the Beef Tribunal, it was suggested that, at the meat plant involved, irregularities were widely acknowledged at almost all ranks in the workforce.

Some observers have suggested that, in the Irish case, the propensity for corruption in these areas is augmented by the level of taxation morality and the source of the funds being misappropriated. On the issue of tax evasion, even when both financially significant and involving politicians, Irish people's judgement may lack severity because more petty transgressions are so widespread. Unethical behaviour, be it in tax evasion, welfare fraud or false claims for compensation, is defended because 'everybody else does it', 'the victims are usually faceless' or the tax system is or was too onerous.[24] The public judgement may also be mitigated, it is suggested, if the victim is not just faceless but an agency of the European Union (EU).

Ethical Leadership

> Corruption was once conceived of in much broader terms than the meanings we employ today. Classical conceptions . . . dealt not with the actions of individuals, but with the moral health of whole societies . . . As the scope of politics has broadened, however, our conceptions of corruption have narrowed . . . There now seems little point in labelling whole polities as corrupt. We thus tend to see corruption as specific actions by specific individuals.[25]

Connected to the explanations of corruption that centre on general public morality are those which single out the lack of exemplary ethical leadership. These suggest that corruption at elite level gives a signal to others that such behaviour is more generally acceptable:

> High level corruption generally renders low level corruption inevitable the tone is set at the top. But the reverse is not true.[26]

This effect is hard to measure but can be fairly obvious in systemic or extreme cases such as the Mugabe regime in Zimbabwe. Several incidents highlighted above suggest that many people in politics and business must have been aware of the Ansbacher scheme for tax evasion, the basis of Haughey's 'fortune' and other examples of dubious behaviour on the part of the Republic's senior leaders.

> The plain people of Ireland were told time beyond number that Haughey was a political thug and still they elected him. And the movers and shakers within the greatest political party this State has known also backed him time and again, despite all they were told and knew themselves . . . Haughey had made himself rich by accepting payments from businessmen and pilfering Fianna Fáil State-funded coffers. Although this was not generally known initially, as the decade progressed it became known to a widening circle of people.[27]

At a more general level, 'stroke' politics was particularly rife in the years when Haughey was leader of Fianna Fáil. Populist, short-term measures were often adopted in an *ad hoc* fashion with little reference to proper procedure or broader policy consideration. In these circumstances, individual ministers, civil servants and business people may have been influenced by the perceived lax ethical standards in high places. The likelihood of decisive moral leadership may also have been inhibited because politicians in receipt of large sums from property developers occupied cabinet positions with responsibility for local government and justice as well as the Department of the Taoiseach.

The DIRT Inquiry may have a similar impact as, together with figures published in 1998 by the Revenue Commissioners, it demonstrates that some extremely high earners were paying less tax than the average compliant PAYE worker. The Revenue survey of 400 individuals with incomes of more than IR£250,000 in the 1993/94 and 1994/95 tax years showed that the average effective tax rate for nearly one fifth of them was less than 20 per cent (*The Irish Times* 27.2.98). For taxpayers in general, the rate was 24 per cent. It is important to note, however, that the DIRT scandal revealed widespread tax evasion by large numbers of business people on quite modest incomes. For example, an audit of the Bank of Ireland branch in the small town Milltown Malbay in 1992 recovered IR£200,000 in unpaid DIRT arising from bogus non-resident accounts held there. But the Revenue subsequently netted a further IR£1.8 million by pursuing the account holders for untaxed income (*The Irish Times*, 8.7.00).

Some explanations of clientelism in Ireland have linked it to Catholicism both at the level of belief and historical experience. The majority religion, it is speculated, encouraged a belief in the usefulness of intermediaries and a sense of distance from the state. Corruption is similarly observed to be higher in the more Catholic states of Europe. The explanation for this phenomenon probably has more to do with levels of economic and political modernisation than sectarian stereotyping. It does not fit easily into the experience of the various German *Länder* for example. Similarly, in Europe all states have experienced periods of corruption.

The religious explanation may, however, suggest that corruption is a particular danger at times of marked social discontinuities when informal social controls are weakened. In the Republic, rapid economic change has ensured that certain professions, such as banking and accountancy, once disproportionately Protestant, are now drawing more widely for members. It may be that traditional attitudes in these sectors inhibited corruption and that these are no longer being transmitted as efficiently between generations. The same could be said of the new business elite. Scandal in the Catholic Church itself may also have discouraged a more forthright moral leadership in that community.

Financing of Political Parties

Elections must be financed, and wealthy interests concerned with legislative outcomes and government policy may be willing to foot the bill. Financial pressures give politicians an incentive to accept payoffs, thus working against the other corruption-reducing effects of competitive elections.[28]

The discussion above on the causes of corruption examined several broad explanations to be found in the comparative politics literature. One important theme, however, deserves special attention because of the frequency with which it occurs in the Republic. This is the alleged link between corruption and the financing of political parties and elections. As Heywood notes:

> Many of the major scandals in democracies in recent years have been linked in some way to campaign and party finance. The democratic political process costs money – in ever increasing amounts.[29]

The political parties need to finance major marketing operations, not just at election time, but to maintain a high profile between formal campaigns. Discussing Britain, Garvan and Kelly suggest that:

> Among those who acknowledge a problem, it is widely agreed that it has two interlocking features: first, that our parties have insufficient revenue to carry out their 'essential' tasks; secondly, that they rely excessively upon corporate and institutional support.[30]

The decreasing role of both volunteer workers and members' subscriptions has made parties more dependent on professional teams and capital-intensive campaign techniques.[31] As Heywood puts it, 'parties are over extended and under-resourced'.[32] Answering its own question, 'Is corruption in Europe rife?', *The Economist* (29.1.00) declared:

> Not really . . . Where Europeans from all quarters of the continent display common frailties is in their lust for cash for their political parties. In most countries, membership fees now barely cover the smallest of costs, let alone the fortunes that can be spent on media

campaigns . . . So European parties snuggle as closely
as ever to businesses.

In Ireland, the frequency of elections and the level of intra-
party competition for higher preference votes between
candidates of the same party exacerbate the problems of
finance. These factors have obliged election contenders to build
up 'war chests' independently of their own party. Though the
electoral logic of individual campaigns has always been evident,
FitzGerald claims that:

> The problem we now face is, of course, a very different
> one. It is the impact of a growing culture of individual-
> ism upon the multi-seat electoral system. As a result of
> this new factor, personal campaigns by candidates –
> always forbidden in the past although not always
> completely prevented – seem to have become accepted,
> or at least tolerated, by the parties . . . This relaxation of
> the discipline required in a multi-seat electoral system
> seems to have led to the emergence of individual
> funding of candidates on a significant scale. (*The Irish
> Times* 29.4.00).

In the absence of adequate state funding, many critics maintain the pressures of party competition create the conditions that
encourage a dependency on business and wealthy individuals.
The 1999 revelations concerning former German Chancellor
Kohl show that even the availability of support from the public
purse may not prevent the soliciting of covert private support.

> . . . both Germany and Italy have substantial state
> funding of political parties and, in the former case,
> radical disclosure laws . . . Yet none of this prevented
> massive cheating by one of the country's two leading
> political parties [in Germany] . . . Italy's experience also
> suggests state funding is no panacea. Its ruling parties
> simply took bribes as well and bought their way back
> into office with wholesale patronage and cronyism. And
> the state funding of the central apparatuses of the
> parties resulted both in massive centralisation of power

> within the parties . . . state funding and controls on
> financing of political parties . . . may indeed make
> corruption more difficult but by no means stop it. (*The
> Irish Times,* 16.5.00)

As the Burke, Flynn and other cases show, Irish politicians
have felt the need to solicit support from wealthy firms and
individuals to finance their electoral campaigns. In the absence
of the tighter regulations that apply today, any donation from
business or other supporters could be categorised by the recipient politicians as 'for electoral purposes'. This designation may
well have facilitated corruption.

Some commentators have seen all private funding as
essentially iniquitous and inevitably corrupt:

> The explanation for the corruption of our political
> system lies in part . . . in the manner in which the system
> is financed. By permitting the private funding of the
> political system, the system is necessarily corrupted.
> Corrupted in the sense of necessarily reflecting the inter-
> ests of its financiers against those of the majority . . .[33]

More tempered views have centred on the role of large
corporate donations both to parties and individuals. The cases
highlighted in Chapter Two suggest that it is at the level of the
individual politician that most suspicion falls. Certainly, it is
more efficient for those who wish to exert influence to seek to
influence the decision-makers directly.

In some senses, 'political expenses are caught in an inflation-
ary spiral especially during election periods'.[34] As discussed
above, in Ireland politicians face an unusually high level of both
intra- and inter-party competition. In addition, their publicity
competes with all-pervasive commercial advertising and they
cannot rely on ideological differences to mobilise broad sections
of the electorate. Though the restrictions on election expenditure
are now stricter than in the 1980s and 1990s, the temptation to
exceed the legal level is always there. The legislation does not

cover money spent outside the official campaign period and, apart from EP, local and by-elections, will be first operational from the next general election.

Political Career Patterns

Della Porta and Vannucci,[35] in analysing corruption in Italy, assign to political parties the roles of 'guarantors' of illegal exchanges, partners in reciprocal protection against scandal and facilitators in the 'socialisation in illegality'. In the Brazilian case, Geddes and Neto interestingly isolate the characteristics of the electoral system as a contributory factor in explaining traditional levels of corruption.[36] They refer particularly to the pressures on politicians to become 'distributors of largesse'.[37] This study of Ireland, however, takes these characteristics to be important principally in cases of systemic corruption, though the differences may be essentially ones of scale. The following gives a flavour of the Italian case:

> . . . on 18 May 1993, only a year after the election of a new parliament . . . 205 out of a total of 630 deputies and 81 out of 326 senators were under investigation, albeit not only for offences against the public administration. By the end of 1994 the number of suspects involved had already reached more than 7000, including 338 ex-deputies, 100 ex-senators, 331 regional, 122 provincial and 1525 communal administrators, and 1373 public functionaries.[38]

The unfolding of the Foley case in 2000 demonstrated how a politician might be much wealthier than his colleagues or electors imagined. The tabloid press tend to suggest that TDs are much richer than their salary scales suggest. According to *Ireland on Sunday:*

> One in every eight Dáil deputies is a millionaire. While some TDs put on the poor mouth with an annual salary of IR£38,000, plus expenses, over 20 others can boast to be millionaires, at least on paper.[39]

Irish candidates are, however, seldom privately wealthy. Even the examples of TDs in the *Ireland on Sunday* article included some whose 'valuation' included their principal residence, assumed potential as heirs to business and other assets. Several months later, the same newspaper's investigative report on ministers concluded:

> There may be a cynical perception that they live in mansions acquired by dubious wealth. But in fact the majority of ministers appear to be plodding along with the rest of the middle classes . . . living in comfortable but relatively unspectacular circumstances. (*Ireland on Sunday*, 16 July 2000)

Most deputies come from mundane middle-class backgrounds and politics is their career. Forty-seven per cent of TDs are from the lower or higher professions; 'by far the most numerous profession in the Dáil is schoolteachers'.[40] This dependence on politics for a livelihood may itself be a danger. Donatella della Porta and Alessandro Pizzorno,[41] in a study of Italy, have talked of 'business politicians':

> . . . a new breed of political entrepreneur who 'combines mediation in (licit or illicit) business transactions, first-hand participation in economic activity, and political mediation in the traditional sense . . . [the] emergence of so-called 'business politicians' . . . reflects a perceived tendency for a growing number to enter politics primarily for personal gain.[42]

There is little evidence that such commercial motives may be present in Ireland though, interestingly, Rose-Ackerman discusses the phenomena in both France and Italy to parties loosing 'ideological focus'.[43] Della Porta makes a related observation:

> The decisive criterion is the system used to legitimise the parties in the eyes of the public. There is a fundamental distinction between legitimisation by symbolic means, i.e. by convincing the electorate that the party is

working for the common good, and legitimisation by material means, which associates membership of a political movement with special access to public funds. The latter approach involves 'buying' votes individually, which considerably increases the expense of politics.[44]

The Irish system of public procurement, auditing and professional bureaucracy does not open sufficient opportunities for 'business politicians' at either central or local government levels. The uncertainty of ministerial appointment for most parliamentarians means that entering politics as a business venture would be highly speculative even if opportunity for rent seeking were available. The crucial exception is in relation to planning. As FitzGerald observes:

Rare, however, are Irish politicians who enter politics with the intention of securing illicit gains. To think otherwise is to misunderstand the nature of political corruption and, if we are to defeat corruption, we need to understand how it operates. It does so not by inserting corrupt people into the system but by corrupting weak people already in the system . . . (*The Irish Times,* 29.4.00)

As the wealthiest TD, the former Taoiseach Albert Reynolds, observed in the *Ireland on Sunday* article:

'I was, actually [shocked at the 'brown envelope' syndrome which affected my party in the 1970s and 1980s]', he sighs. 'I had no whisper of it at all. I just couldn't believe it, to be quite honest with you.' . . . He admits that some TDs today may be open to overtures from big business. 'I wouldn't like to be in politics and be dependent solely on politics', he says. 'I think it would have affected me during my years as minister and indeed as Taoiseach; it would have affected my decision-making if I had to look over my shoulder, wondering whether I was going to be out of a job or, you know, if that decision was going to be the end of a career and not having anything to fall back on.'[45]

The pattern of political careers is characterised by much more stability than the rhetoric of democratic competition suggests. Over 77 per cent of deputies have been in the Dáil for ten years or more.[46]

Some observers have linked the pressures of a political career and corruption to the use of politics as a vehicle for social advancement.

> . . . a political career is seen as a particularly rapid way of climbing the social ladder, especially since there is a growing interaction between the political and business worlds, giving rise to a proliferation of go-betweens who do not fully belong to either and therefore find it easier to break the rules of both. The rewards of political life are necessarily material and undisclosed.[47]

There is a tendency for Irish politicians to avoid any suggestion of social distance between themselves and their electorate. Nevertheless, political office, whether local or national, does have social cachet. It provides opportunities for those with social aspirations to mix with members of the commercial or social elite that might not otherwise be available. Such social mobility is not confined to those whose origins are notably humble, though the potential distance travelled may be greater.

Conclusions

To understand the causes of corruption in the Republic's politics, it is important to see the phenomenon as similar to that in other states. The specific roots may be in Irish experience but the form of corruption is comparable. Corruption in Ireland is not new. As elsewhere it is associated with levels of partisan competition, state activity, bureaucratic discretion and the system of party finance. Other jurisdictions have similar forms of corruption though some can be seen to be more facilitating. Similarly, Chapter Four will analyse the consequences of corruption in the context of experience elsewhere.

4. The Consequences of Corruption in Ireland

If the Republic follows the pattern of Italy, France and other liberal democracies, initial indignation at revelations of corruption, unquestioned support for those leading the investigations and popular opprobrium directed at those implicated will give way to rueful acceptance of the status quo and impatience with the anti-corruption process. Judges, campaigning journalists and others involved in the reform effort will make errors of judgement and revisionists will suggest less harsh verdicts on those caught up in corruption.

> C'est la France jacobine qui a fait de la justice une simple 'autorité' soumise au pouvoir politique . . . Faute pour les politiques de s'en être aperçus à temps, les juges on décrété leur indépendance. Dans la foulée de la révolution italienne de 'Mani Pulite' . . . ils ont, pour affirmer leur pouvoir, utilisé toutes les ressources du droit pénal . . . L'indépendance de la justice est une nécessité démocratique. Mais, d'une absence dommageable de pouvoir, la justice risque de verser dans un excès de pouvoir. (*Le Monde*, 3.11.99).

It is important, therefore, to make clear the impact of corruption on the political system. Following Hope,[1] three types of consequences of corruption are isolated:

 a. economic;
 b. political; and,
 c. administrative.

Individually and collectively, each of these has a negative impact on the Republic of Ireland.

Economic

There is a literature that suggests that corruption can have positive outcomes.

> Corruption has apologists. Some countries . . . have deserved reputations for corruption, and yet have

> grown fast. Economists have argued that corruption can increase economic efficiency in some areas . . . On balance, the evidence supports the proposition that corruption is damaging.[2]

Arguments favouring corruption are disregarded here because they occur in political systems that are systemically corrupt or hopelessly inefficient.

> Corruption is a major obstacle to economic development. It reduces domestic investment, discourages foreign direct investment, inflates government spending, and shifts government spending away from education, health and infrastructure maintenance towards less efficient (more manipulable) public projects.[3]

The most direct economic consequence of corruption is to make business more costly. Rent-seeking behaviour by politicians or officials adds to the expense of business, diverts expenditure from other uses, increases taxes and causes macroeconomic distortion. The allocation of local monopolies to suppliers of services with high initial costs, such as cable television, is fraught with economic dangers. Corruption may lead to the awards of licences, which are not based on intrinsic economic considerations. Customers and/or taxpayers eventually carry the cost.

International action encouraged by the World Bank, OECD and others has sought to put legal barriers on businesses that might resort to bribery in foreign markets. Most famously, the Foreign Corruption Practices Act, 1977 exposes American companies to prosecution in the US for corruption abroad. Maybe as a result, Americans are quick to point the finger at others. For example, George Soros, the Hungarian-American author of in *The Crisis of Global Capitalism*, claims that the EU is too forgetful about the problem of corruption.[4]

> Western governments had for too long been prepared to tolerate it, viewing it as the price to be paid for political stability . . . There is always somebody who pays, and international business is generally the main source of corruption (*Financial Times*, 17.3.00)

More recently, former CIA director James Woolsey accused European companies of using wholesale bribery to win international contracts.

> . . . European companies were involved in international bribery because their economies were dominated by governments making European firms less able to reduce costs and adapt quickly to economic circumstances. (*Financial Mail on Sunday*, 23.5.00)

The Transparency Index, along with other risk assessments, allows businesses to measure the perceived level of corruption in all the significant economies in the world.

> [The Index] suggests that the poorer the country, the more corrupt. It tends to be the richest countries that are the least corrupt. The match is not perfect, but it is close . . . This does not demonstrate that countries are poor because they are corrupt. Causation might run the other way, countries are corrupt because they are poor. Probably, it is a bit of both. But what is certain is that corruption varies among countries with similar incomes per head – and does significant damage to economic performance.[5]

The Transparency Index is, of course, an indirect measure of corruption. Nevertheless, it does allow Irish corruption to be put into a comparative framework. With the exception of the export credits for beef, the passport affair and the use of offshore banks, the Irish cases cited above seldom involve foreign companies or international trade. It may be that the position of multinational investors and businesses has been so strong relative to Ireland that they have been able to resist rent-seeking

TABLE 4.1: Ranking of a Selection of Countries on the
Corruption Perception Index

Ranking	Country	Indicator
1	Finland	10.0
2	Denmark	9.8
3	New Zealand	9.4
	Sweden	9.4
5	Canada	9.2
6	Iceland	9.1
	Norway	9.1
	Singapore	9.1
9	Netherlands	8.9
10	United Kingdom	8.7
11	Luxembourg	8.6
	Switzerland	8.6
13	Australia	8.3
14	USA	7.8
15	Austria	7.7
	Hong Kong	7.7
17	Germany	7.6
18	Chile	7.4
19	Ireland	7.2
20	Spain	7.01

Unit: On a scale of 0 to 10 where '0' refers to a country where business transactions are
entirely penetrated by corruption and '10' indicates a perfectly 'clean' country.

Coverage: 2000. Source: Transparency International, 2000. Ireland in 1999 was 15th (7.7)

demands from corrupt politicians or public servants. Alternatively such attempts have not been made. International investors qualify for substantial grants and a favourable tax regime in the Republic.

In relation to international trade, the Republic has not featured in comparative empirical investigations. One such study of eighteen major trading companies concludes, however, that, in relation to responsibility for corruption:

> . . . exporting countries do not simply take the cultural climate as given and adjust their ethical standards accordingly. In so far as export behaviour differs across nations, the inclination to offer bribes emerges as the sovereign choice of exporters.[6]

The international perception of Ireland's level of corruption has altered but not as much as anticipated in the light of recent revelations. The impact on actual inward investment is impossible to assess in the absence of direct evidence from foreign companies. Domestically, corruption may well have unfairly provided opportunities for some businesses and frustrated others. The major areas of concern are in development planning, broadcasting and tax designation for urban development. Similarly, the furtive nature of various tax evasion schemes lead to flight of capital and lower levels of domestic investment, even though the yields from foreign financial investment may have been repatriated. It is ironic that the fear of capital flight is offered as a major reason for the authorities' failure to act against bogus non-resident accounts.

Political

The second area of concern about the consequence of corruption is its impact on the political system itself. In cases of systemic corruption, dramatic, regime-threatening consequences can be witnessed involving revolutions, repression and coups. The process of national development may be undermined or parallel structures based on the black economy, gangsterism or traditional society arise. These are not within the range of the magnitude that is relevant in Ireland. The analysis offered here would not support Vincent Browne's contention that:

> It isn't just a handful of local councillors who are corrupt; the political system is corrupt . . . All the main political parties have been deeply infected by this, and a large proportion of the population have been gravely disadvantaged by it. (*The Irish Times*, 3.5.00)

Political consequences may, however, be usefully examined for public participation, political recruitment and political accountability.

Public participation

> One reason is that corruption inhibits the growth of autonomous groups within civil society – organisations

> and interests loyal to the system, but enjoying a healthy
> independence from the state, from political patrons, and
> from each other. By creating dependency and/or
> exploitative relationships between politically powerful
> figures, on the one hand, and private citizens on the
> other, corruption weakens civil society and renders citi-
> zens less able to influence and balance the state.[7]

The political systems of liberal democracies depend in part
on a relatively low level of actual participation but a high belief
in its potential efficacy. This arrangement in turn rests on significant levels of trust in politicians, public servants and other
authority figures.

> An open, responsive and effective political process
> requires, at a minimum, a significant amount of citizen
> trust in officials, in institutions, and in each other. Open
> politics means not only that people are free to advocate
> vigorously their own interests, but also that they abide
> by official decisions, accepting unfavourable outcomes
> as fundamentally legitimate and mounting their
> responses through the political process. It also means
> that people trust others to do likewise, for there is little
> reason to play by the rules if one's critics and opponents
> are unlikely to do so too . . . In addition to its material
> costs, one of the primary political costs of corruption is
> that it undermines and can destroy this political trust.[8]

Liberal democracy is especially dependent on public trust.[9]
McAllister's observations are, therefore, particularly worrying:

> In almost every advanced society, voters' trust in their
> politicians has reached historic lows in recent years . . .
> In no democratic country is the trend stable, let alone
> showing greater confidence: the only question is the
> rapidity with which the decline in public political confi-
> dence is taking place.[10]

In Ireland, though there has been a decline in voter participation particularly since the 1980s, trust in political institutions is

relatively high. In the 1999 Spring Standard Eurobarometer 51, respondents were asked to state their trust or distrust in their national and international institutions. On average 35 per cent of Europeans trust the civil service, the Parliament, the government and the political parties of their country. The country results show that average trust levels range from 25 per cent in Italy to 56 per cent in the Netherlands. The Irish score was 39 per cent. When disaggregated, however, it is clear that trust in the civil service (61 per cent) is much greater than in political parties (21 per cent).

Perhaps a more telling indication of trust is the finding in April 2000 that 46 per cent of the respondents to an IMS opinion poll indicated they did not believe the Taoiseach's denial that he received IR£50,000 from a Cork businessman in 1989. The poll showed 36 per cent accepted Ahern's word while 18 per cent expressed no opinion. Interestingly, 67 per cent of those polled approved of the Taoiseach's leadership (*Sunday Independent*, 30.4.00). Re-establishing public trust once it has been seriously eroded is very difficult.

A recent survey of 18- o 24-year-olds asked: 'Would the recent tribunals and their revelations deter you from voting?' Seventy per cent of respondents said yes; of these, 50 per cent had voted in the local and European elections 1999.[11] Political participation may be eroded by corruption if measured by voter turnout or party membership. There may, however, be less impact if the gauge was direct action, pressure group membership or the formation of new political groupings. By each of these measures, Ireland may not be seeing an overall decline in political participation. There is, however, a telling lack of empirical evidence.

Political recruitment

The primary agents for political recruitment in liberal democracies are political parties. Successful independent candidates are few even in systems that do not operate on a party-list basis for elections. Of the candidates in the 1997 Irish general election, 21 per cent were independents but they secured less than 4 per cent of the seats. Political parties generally recruit from a sub-set of their membership who are characterised by a willingness to stand, social circumstances that facilitate holding office and the criteria that other members expect elected members to meet. In most countries, this has led to disproportionately male, middle-aged and middle-class cohorts from a relatively narrow range of professions holding office. In systemic cases, as della Porta and Vanucci demonstrate in Italy:

> The corrupt party provides socialisation to the rules of the (illegal) game, permitting the system of covert trans-actions to expand. Politicians already 'introduced' to the rules of the illegal market place introduce others in their turn.[12]

If, as is not the case, the process of political recruitment in the Republic operated on a similar basis, for a significant number of politicians this would fulfil the criteria for institutional corruption.

The recruitment of more women into politics may have a positive impact on corruption. According to studies summarised by Transparency International (1999):

> Higher levels of women's participation in public life are associated with lower levels of corruption. Corruption is less severe where women comprise a larger share of parliamentary seats . . . [Further] higher rates of female participation in government are associated with lower levels of corruption . . .

As well as having a lower propensity for corruption while holding public office, research suggests that:

> Women in business seem less likely to pay bribes . . . firms owned or managed by women pay bribes on approximately 5% of occasions when coming into contact with a government agency. The percentage is twice as high for firms with a male owner or manager (11%).[13]

Political accountability

> The revelation of widespread corruption [in Italy and other European nations after the Cold War] helped undermine one of the support structures – the claim to operate on the basis of public accountability which had underpinned western democracies in the post-war world.[14]

Public accountability in Ireland operates, at central government level, through the doctrines of individual and collective responsibility of ministers and other members to parliament. By extension, Oireachtas members are answerable to the electorate. As Geddes and Neto note:

> Ultimately . . . accountability depends on something more basic [than the idiosyncrasies of a particular political system]: the public's desire and ability to end the political careers of corrupt officeholders.[15]

The Irish electorate have been relatively lenient. For example, Lowry topped the poll in North Tipperary in 1997 even after revelations about receiving payments from Dunne and tax evasion. Notwithstanding the voters' ambiguity, the role of periodic elections is too broad to be an effective instrument of public accountability. As McAllister puts it:

> . . . the principle of 'throwing the rascals out' . . . assumes that electors are sufficiently well informed . . . [and] will be able to overcome their partisan loyalties, by perhaps voting against their favoured party in order to remove an unsatisfactory elected representative.[16]

In the simple model of parliamentary accountability, the focus for an assessment of corruption is properly the Dáil and its committees. In recognition of this, members have a level of immunity from prosecution and they cannot be sued for remarks made there.[17]

> In most countries, legislators enjoy some form of immu-
> nity from civil and/or criminal prosecution. There are
> two types of legislative immunity. The more limited type
> of immunity is 'non-liability' – in which legislators
> cannot be detained or prosecuted for votes cast and
> opinions expressed while carrying out legislative duties.
> Ireland, the United Kingdom and the United States limit
> legislative immunity to this type.[18]

Although parliamentarians elsewhere have more general protection, Dáil deputies still protect their privilege. Thus, for example, in the recent case involving Deputy Foley, a Dáil committee adjudicated on his conduct and its recommendation of a thirty-day suspension was accepted by the Dáil. Similarly, Minister Burke made his initial response to accusations of corruption in a statement on the floor of the chamber. The weakness of parliamentary control was, however, pinpointed by Deputy Jim Mitchell, chairman of the Public Accounts Committee and the DIRT inquiry:

> . . . all the scandals have a common strand. All of them
> represent a failure of political and parliamentary
> accountability. (*The Irish Times*, 17.12.99)

If the legislature was working effectively, both through its elected members and their political staff, the system would be so transparent and accountable that political corruption should be minimal. The rise of more disciplined parties, the increased pace of the legislative process and the wider remit of government have, however, militated against incisive parliamentary scrutiny. These factors are particularly acute in political systems such as Ireland's in which members of the legislature fill the cabinet and other government offices. The political fortunes of parliamentarians are closely linked to the popularity of the senior members of their party in the executive. This has led to the accusation that Dáil investigations are 'soft' on ministers:

> Former ministers for finance came in for very little crit-
> icism in the DIRT report of the Committee of Public

Accounts . . . The softness with which politicians were treated . . . contrasts with its treatment of civil servants and bankers, a point which is of added relevance in the context of the committee's overall hope that Oireachtas committees might replace tribunals as the vehicle for investigating controversies of public significance (*The Irish Times*, 18.12.99)

Despite measures such as the Committees of the Houses of the Oireachtas (Compellability, Privileges and Immunities of Witnesses) Act, 1997, critics suspect that the odds against the detection of corruption are lengthening. In recognition of similar misgivings, many parliamentary systems augment the role of the legislature with other watchdog agencies such as ombudsmen, special prosecutors and other quasi-judicial bodies. In Ireland, it is a feature of several incidents cited above that Dáil deputies were unable to elicit crucial information, which was subsequently central to tribunal and other inquiries.

The appointment of tribunals and inquiries on the foot of media revelations of corruption is a recognition that the established means of public accountability have been deficient. It is difficult to assess whether this was as a consequence of corruption, though the revelations about Deputy Foley indicate the potential dangers. It is unlikely that the corrupt parliamentarian would ask the difficult question which might expose another and/or endanger him or herself. Similarly, it is those who hold cabinet office who have the greatest opportunities for illicit rent seeking. The Irish parliamentary system, like cognate ones elsewhere, is very much dominated by the government. This is not as a result of corruption but it is in the interests of the corrupt to resist more effective methods of parliamentary scrutiny. Further, those who sought to use parliamentary methods to highlight corruption were harried and characterised as unpatriotic.

The safeguard of collective responsibility was undermined by corruption. The doctrine is supposed to make cabinet colleagues sensitive to each other's decisions because any one member is obliged to defend publicly every policy. It is now clear that there were grounds to doubt the probity of a recent Taoiseach and other senior ministers but their colleagues failed to act. The flaw may be the dominance of the Taoiseach in a cabinet of career politicians. Alternatively, it may be that the pressure of individual departmental responsibilities did not allow time for a truly collective approach.

It is hardly in the interests of back-bench parliamentarians from parties in government to question ministers so resolutely that they undermine their collective electoral credibility. Private party meetings, therefore, assume a significant role in the system of parliamentary accountability. During Haughey's tenure as prime minister, party forums were important but not sufficient checks.

In local government, the elected council as a whole is the accountable body but, in larger local authorities, committees also play a key role. At this level, the county or city manager also provides a regular account of his actions at open public meetings of the council in a way that has only recently been paralleled in central government. In the terms used here and with the major exception of planning, corruption in local government is incidental.

Administrative

As always in studies of corruption, the analysis must start by noting that the activity is secretive and covert. It is impossible to know whether the corruption that is exposed is representative or not. An unknowable amount will remain hidden. In Ireland, the legislation used to govern corruption had until recently changed little for almost eighty years. Under the Public Bodies Corrupt Practices Act, 1889, and the Prevention of Corruption Acts 1906 and 1916, bribery of a public official leaves both giver and receiver open to a seven-year prison sentence. The Ethics in Public Office Act, 1995, updated the law and shifted the burden of proof in some cases. Thus, where senior government or parliamentary office holders are involved, money is deemed to be given corruptly unless proven otherwise. The 1995 Act has made conviction much easier. On the other hand, exposure of corruption through the media is inhibited by relatively high burdens of proof in the law on defamation. According to Frank McDonald, *The Irish Times* environment correspondent: 'At any given time in the last 10 years of Dublin County Council, I could have named at least 12 members who were irredeemably corrupt.' He makes the same claim in relation to officials. (*The Irish Times*, 3.5.00)

After independence, the Free State bureaucracy retained the centralising features of its British predecessor. The enormous importance of the civil service and local authorities, and, to a lesser extent, the state-sponsored bodies was heightened by the dominance of the public sector in the rather underdeveloped post-independence economy. Because of its political indispensability, the civil service was able to retain its corporate integrity and identity, and to resist pressures towards politicisation. The recruitment and promotion procedures of the Irish public service are formally and rigorously meritocratic. Political appointments as special advisers to ministers are few and, notwithstanding the Duffy incident, seldom controversial. They end when governments change.

Traditionally, the civil service has stressed equity, impartiality and integrity as their key assets. Today, these are still important but a number of other criteria have been identified as part of the 'new public management' (NPM) trend. It is widely recognised that the traditional management structure did not encourage individuals to take personal responsibility. NPM stresses the achievement of targets, performance indicators and, in some countries, payment by results. Some fear that this new environment will encourage some public servants to be less responsive to the traditional norms that inhibited corruption.

Partly as a safeguard against the abuse of bureaucratic power, several legislative changes have been made to the 1920s statutes that entrenched the Republic's British-style system of public administration. For example, in April 1998 the Freedom of Information Act came into effect. This gives the public access to official records, files and reports of government departments and public bodies. The legislation effectively overturns the presumption that all official information is secret. Some data, especially commercially sensitive or legally privileged material, are excluded from the scope of the Act. Further, a Supreme Court decision, also in April 1998, widened the right of the media to report court cases and clarified the public's rights to information. To augment the established parliamentary process, the Office of the Ombudsman was established in Ireland in 1980. The Ombudsman investigates complaints against a range of public authorities. Similarly, the Comptroller and Auditor General has been given wider powers in recent years to examine the effectiveness as well as the probity of public spending.

State-industry relations that obscure the separation between public and private interests may compromise political accountability and facilitate corruption. This danger has been recognised in corporatist institutional arrangements of the type found in several small European countries. These bring together business, labour and government in a concerted effort to establish consensus on major economic policies. Corporatist agreements between the 'social partners' in Ireland, such as the Programme for Prosperity and Fairness (PPF), Partnership 2000 and the Programme for Competitiveness and Work are credited with underpinning economic growth. These arrangements between government and civil society have become quite extensive and, as well as employers and unions, include agricultural, voluntary, social and other interests. Critics allege that they may blur the distinction between public and private interests because certain interests are afforded a direct role in political decisions. They almost inevitably decrease the involvement of parliament in policy formation and supervision.

> There can be no doubt about the contribution that
> successive national partnership agreements have made

to our economic and social progress . . . more than 35 new bodies are to be established at national level, almost all involving participation by social partners . . . All this raises a question, however, about the nature, role, and quality of representative democracy in our State. The matters contained in this programme are the very stuff of traditional politics: they are precisely the kind of things that one expects to see addressed in political party manifestos and to hear regularly debated in parliament...Now, however, they are discussed, argued about, and finally agreed . . . by consensus among what are called the social partners. [V]ery few politicians . . . are conscious of this shift away from traditional representative democracy and towards a new, and it has to be said, thus far largely benevolent form of corporatism.[19]

The process of managing conflicting social and economic interests through corporatism has in other jurisdictions facilitated corruption. By granting privileged roles, corporatism creates the potential for rent creation. The notion of 'cosy cartels', 'golden circles' or 'cronyism' is a frequent feature of the cases sketched out above. The financial accounts of family members and political parties have also been subject to investigation. Gifts, easy loans or preferential business opportunities may not be illegal but may be corrupt, according to the definition adopted in this study.

Ownership or direct supervision of certain enterprises by the state can compromise the neutrality of public officials even in open democratic societies based on a predominantly market economy. Such a conflict can seem very immediate for civil servants charged with inspecting individual enterprises, such as Department of Agriculture personnel at meat plants, who may form very close relations with the employees. In recognition of this danger senior civil servants told the Dáil Public Accounts Committee (6 June 1999):

> We have had a system for some time now of rotating staff at plant level . . . [However] if one is moving people on a regular basis one has to give them removal expenses. What we have been doing is rotating staff on a temporary basis. The staff in our meat plants have one day a month in a different plant. Speaking from memory, we have put about 60 or 70 new staff into meat plants, effectively to replace staff that were already there.

It is important to be aware that there is a constant danger that in circumstances of discretion and ineffective supervision corruption can occur. This is exacerbated when there is political pressure for swift action and simpler procedures. Such recognition may help the development of effective risk management techniques.

5. Anti-Corruption Strategies

The recognition that political corruption is an increasingly serious problem for liberal democracies has led most such states to introduce co-ordinated anti-corruption strategies. These are generally informed by the academic literature reviewed in previous chapters.

One benefit of an analytical approach to corruption is the ability it offers to assess the scale of the phenomenon. Anti-corruption strategies, however, are often imbued with the sense of scandal felt by the electorate about particular events. For this reason, they may fail to deal effectively with the problem. As the Public Offices Commission states in its *Annual Report* for 1999 (p. 12):

> It is . . . important . . . that the backlash against those in public service, which understandably may arise as a result of the revelations at the Tribunals of Inquiry, does not result in a[n anti-corruption] code which is so excessively technical that it may hinder rather than support the main objective of ensuring acceptance of

> and commitment to the fundamental principle of
> honesty in public life . . . The degree of supervision
> should not, as may have happened in some other coun-
> tries, become part of the problem. Ethics regimes
> generally should not be seen as a collection of reactive
> rules designed to punish unsuspecting participants . . .

In Ireland, there is no doubt that there is a major sense of scandal and hurt among electors. The overwhelming majority of Irish people had no idea before the revelations of the recent tribunals of the amount of corruption, the money involved or the range of business and political figures implicated. In an atmosphere of scandal, many now assert that all politicians, planners, developers and public servants have been guilty of corruption. Often this assertion is modified when particularly popular politicians are named but the general accusation is still affirmed. This pessimistic verdict is given in the context of other scandals that have undermined the Church, the medical estab-lishment and other caring professions. As yet, public opinion is not ready for the suggestion that comparatively the Republic has low levels of corruption or that it is confined to relatively few policy areas. To use the analogy of disease, the Irish public is convinced that the Republic is undergoing an epidemic rather than a disturbing but confirmed outbreak of a predictable common illness. Similarly, not all corruption is equally serious or pernicious. As Klitgaard notes:

> Corruption that undercuts the rules of the game – for
> example, the justice system, or property rights, or
> banking and credit – devastates economic and political
> development. Corruption that allows polluters to foul
> rivers or hospitals to extort exorbitant or improper
> payments from patients can be environmentally and
> socially corrosive. In comparison, providing some speed
> money to get quicker access to public services and
> engaging in mild irregularities in campaign financing
> are less damaging.[1]

In an atmosphere of scandal or righteous indignation, strategies for dealing with corruption are open to misjudgements that may deter citizens from becoming active in politics individually, as party members, or through pressure groups. The public mood may support harsher and more stringent measures than may be useful. A 'zero tolerance' approach may also encourage the belief that corruption can be eradicated rather than controlled. As noted earlier, it may undermine the level of trust upon which liberal democracy depends. Further, the cost of such an approach could become unsustainable in both absolute and opportunity terms. The public already resents the legal bills associated with the various tribunals and inquiries currently in train.

Strategy Choices

> . . . governments should not be fatalistic or passive about corruption. With well-focused and determined efforts, corruption can be reduced, though not to zero. Trying to bring corruption to zero would be too costly in terms of resources and in other ways . . . Any realistic strategy must start with an explicit recognition that there are those who demand acts of corruption on the part of public sector employees and there are public employees willing for a price to perform these acts.[2]

The range of strategies for dealing with corruption is wide. Some have a vicarious appeal to those most offended or shocked by the misuse of public office. The example of China, where corrupt officials and party members are occasionally executed after brief court appearances, has often been cited. The effective choices for Ireland probably stop some way short of the People's Republic's option. Executions have not been wholly effective in dealing with China's corruption. Most western anti-corruption strategies are based on more than one measure and they stress prevention. As an OECD survey found:

> . . . law enforcement, investigation and control measures with strong sanctions attached were regarded

by most countries as essential to prevent corruption. These were followed by preventative and educative approaches such as financial and management controls and training . . . Among the new initiatives against corruption reported by countries, moves to increase administrative transparency stood out as the most popular. In particular, obliging public officials to declare financial and other interests . . . A new direction is discernible . . . streamlining excessive or irrelevant regulation, targeting high-risk areas of government activity, and ensuring financial and banking regulation. This kind of approach . . . looking beyond individual corrupt transactions to the conditions that allow corruption to develop . . .[3]

Drawing on Riley's[4] summary of the political science literature, the following forms of anti-corruption strategy will be discussed:

a.   international;
b.   national;
c.   local; and,
d.   populist.

International

According to a World Bank estimate:

> . . . the sums distributed worldwide each year as 'pay-offs' or 'bribes' total US$80 billion. Given that much of bribery and corruption goes undetected this figure probably represents 'the tip of the iceberg'.[5]

The cases reviewed in Chapter Two suggest that Ireland has not been an 'importer' of corruption though the state's development strategy has stressed the attraction of investment from abroad. The Republic has been supportive of international efforts to combat corruption – of particular importance has been the OECD. Ireland is one of thirty four signatory states, which includes all the world's biggest economies, to the Convention on

Combating Bribery of Foreign Public Officials in International Business Transactions. The Convention makes it a crime to bribe foreign officials and ends tax deductibility for bribe payments. A monitoring procedure is in place. Although the Republic has yet to be assessed, there is a commitment to these international efforts through the OECD that will mean Irish strategies should be compatible with other countries.

> The Convention obliges signatories to adopt national legislation that makes it a crime to bribe foreign public officials . . . punishable, by effective, proportionate and dissuasive criminal penalties comparable to those applicable to their own public officials. . .[6]

Although multinationals have not been a focus for corruption in Ireland, the EU has. Franz-Hermann Bruener, Director General of the EU's anti-fraud office, OLAF, suggests that new strategies need better access to member state's files, Union-wide anti-fraud rules and common penalties for offenders.[7]

Ireland has subscribed to anti-corruption measures brought forward by the World Trade Organisation (WTO), World Bank, IMF, Council of Europe and others. The WTO, for example, notes that globally most bribe-givers are from the First World and most recipients from the Third. The international corruption debate often follows an American agenda partly in response to the pressure US companies are under from their domestic legislation, notably the Foreign Corrupt Practices Act, 1977. The most visible international group, however, has been Transparency International. This NGO publishes the index of corruption on which Table 4.1 is based. The index measures the perceptions of business people of corruption in foreign countries. Despite the technical drawbacks of a perception index, Transparency International's figures are presented by the media as a league table of corruption and, as such, they impact on national strategies.

In several parts of the world, states have co-operated in initiatives to diagnose corruption. Often this effort has arisen from a recognition of limited research resources and has occurred mainly in developing nations. In Ireland, however, such co-operation could usefully form part of the Good Friday Agreement–inspired links between the parliamentary and government institutions in these islands. An advantage to such co-operation would be the institutional similarities at both governmental and professional levels.

National Strategies

The analysis above suggests that corruption in Ireland is associated with discretion in public policies that allow particular and significant benefits to small numbers of individuals. One clear strategy, therefore, is to reduce the number of occasions on which discretion can be exercised. Economists suggest that this implies controlling rent-seeking opportunities. In practice, this may be achieved by flattening the decision-making process and time-limiting the power of politicians and officials. In the particularly susceptible areas, such as planning permissions and agricultural supports, this strategy may, for example, assume that most applicants for minor decisions had been successful unless refusal had come in a short time. It would also reduce the number of levels at which approvals need to be sought. Such a strategy would 'design out' corruption through the presumption of good faith on the part of citizens and a clarification of the limits of official or political discretion. However, it should be recognised that the main problems are in the context of major new investments and material contraventions of the Development Plan.

Anti-corruption strategies in the Republic would have to address the perception of patronage in appointments. Governments will continue to make appointments that ensure that their political judgements are reflected in the major decisions of public bodies. Such appointments encourage some level of compliance with ministerial policy imperatives. Because ministers face the political odium for failed policies, even when the decisions are rightly those of nominated boards, political appointments are likely to continue. Already, many of these appointments are circumscribed by understandings with the social partners. It would be appropriate, however, to increase Dáil oversight through a process of parliamentary ratification. This strategy would strengthen public confidence that the appointments reflected merit criteria as well as political sympathies.

> Few countries in the world have investigated political corruption, maladministration and tax evasion with such zeal as Ireland is now doing . . . At issue is public confidence in the integrity of our democracy . . . The work of the Public Accounts Committee (PAC), in investigating the non-payment of DIRT taxes, has been critical in this regard . . . [T]he PAC exposed tax evasion on a grand scale.[8]

The case for increasing parliamentary oversight of policy as a counter to corruption was greatly helped by the role of the PAC in the inquiry into DIRT. The committee was well resourced, cross-party and narrowly focussed. Any national-level strategy must include steps to augment parliamentary oversight.

To enhance its own standing, the Dáil should limit the outside employment of ministers, senior civil servants and special advisers during and for a period after their tenure. It should also bar deputies from acting as lobbyists even when this role is openly declared. Problems can arise if the public feel that access to privileged information has been abused or connections have been used to exert undue influence over government decisions. Similarly, while the increased obligation to disclose personal assets has improved transparency, the Dáil should require the reporting of liabilities, if not publicly, at least to some office in a position to blow the whistle if conflicts of interest occur.

As several minor incidents have shown, receiving gifts can prove embarrassing for politicians, even when they are genuinely an expression of respect or gratitude. On occasion, gifts, including those from wealthy friends, can appear to be a *quid pro quo* for political favours. Similar dilemmas are associated with the acceptance of travel expenses. An Irish anti-corruption strategy in these areas should be sensitive to the need for acceptable hospitality but the benefit of the doubt should always be given to probity.

The Freedom of Information (FoI) Act, 1997, is much more liberal than legislation currently in force elsewhere. In relation to central government, many public bodies, local authorities and health boards, it gives the public access to official records, files and reports. Its remit should be widened to cover other areas where officials or politicians exercise discretion over public resources. Some commercially sensitive or legally privileged material may have to remain excluded from the scope of the Act. Nevertheless, the rights of the public to information should be extended.

The Ethics in Public Office Act, 1995, requires politicians and public servants alike to make disclosures of personal interests which may affect them in the performance of official duties. The Electoral Acts, 1997 and 1998, provide for the disclosure of political donations and election expenditure and expenses. A credible national anti-corruption strategy must assess the impact of this legislation in the light of both public cynicism and the danger of inhibiting further participation in politics.

As suggested in Chapter Four, political parties are central to liberal democracy. The complexities of government demand more responsible and sophisticated parties. A national anti-corruption strategy should not undermine them. A mechanism needs to be put in place to permit both public and private funding of parties as well as individual candidates.

FitzGerald (*The Irish Times*, 17.1.98) points to the clear dangers in this strategy:

• business people may expect private benefit from contributions;
• public opinion is cynical about the motives of private contributors; and,
• politicians may avoid implementing policies to which contributors might be opposed.

Foreign experience suggests, however, that a completely publicly funded party system is hard to police. Further, it may reduce the independence of individuals or groups within parties who are out of step with the party leadership. As former Fianna Fáil dissident and now Minister for Finance, Charlie McCreevy observed in an interview with a provincial newspaper:

> If that [a ban on corporate donations to individuals] was the situation and with the kind of problems I had in Fianna Fáil during the 1980s, I wouldn't be in the Dáil now because I was on the outside . . . I really was *persona non grata* nationally and somewhat locally. So if that was the case I definitely wouldn't have got elected because I wouldn't have been given a fair crack of the whip. (*The Nationalist*, 30.6.00)

Funding for political parties will always be subject to public parsimony. Under-funding encourages illicit or indirect support and less policy research. It is clear from other countries that a dearth of funds diminishes further the stature of political parties and increases their susceptibility to accept donations from dubious business people. Any new system would have to feature full disclosure of contributions.

The Beef Tribunal demonstrated that EU funds had been misused. Major improvements in the administration of the CAP have since been made. EU fines have been reduced. The current strategies for reducing corruption in relation to the CAP include an enhanced inspectorate to ensure compliance with EU regulations, risk management techniques and rotating staff at plant level. Other measures that might apply more widely in the civil service are efficient accountability mechanisms; workable codes of conduct and ethics training. Encouragingly, a code of conduct for all civil servants is being prepared.

Some disquiet remains after the Beef Tribunal and other inquiries about the relationship between business and former public servants. It is significant, therefore, that the new code envisages a cooling-off period before senior civil servants can transfer to parallel positions in the private sector. The code will be all the more timely as the seven years tenure rule for top posts will soon ensure a large pool of relatively young former civil servants becoming available for employment. Restrictions should also be extended to state agencies that claim to be independent of direct government control.

In framing new rules for public servants, it is important to resolve the potential contradiction in current public service reforms between a strict centralised compliance-based ethics infrastructure and devolved results-based management systems. In other jurisdictions, the break up of the single-structured civil service has led to different organisational cultures developing. Not all the new 'ventures' share the same ethical criteria either as each other or the older structure. In treating people as 'customers' it is possible to forget that they are also 'citizens'.

Carol Coulter, legal affairs correspondent of *The Irish Times*, also pointed to a contradiction between the demands of differing systems, i.e. the partisan political world and the independent judiciary.

> If there is agreement on little else, there is agreement that the appointment of Mr Hugh O'Flaherty to the European Investment Bank was a political appointment, made by the majority party in Government to a man who had years of party loyalty behind him. However, no one has drawn attention to the fact that as a member of the judiciary he had left these political associations behind him. Re-establishing them through this appointment carries the risk of affecting public perceptions of the judiciary as a whole. (*The Irish Times*, 30.5.00)

The Supreme Court Judge, Mrs Justice Susan Denham, expressed further misgivings about the impact of the Sheedy controversy on public perceptions of the judiciary:

> . . . modern systems of accountability are not incompatible with judicial independence . . . [The Sheedy case was the] most serious constitutional crisis involving the

> judiciary since the foundation of the State. (*Irish Examiner*, 15.7.00)

Justice Denham, while acknowledging that the Oireachtas retains the power of impeachment, called for new structures to be put in place for dealing with cases of lesser misconduct by judges.

Recent tax-evasion scandals have highlighted the problem of allowing professional groups to be self-regulating. Auditors and other accountants are, like the judges, being asked to consider a new body with wider powers to oversee their operations, punish misconduct and offer a bigger role to those outside the profession to investigate complaints. The new accountancy body would involve the state but would remain responsible to the profession. It is possible, however, that the public may have lost patience with any substantial reliance on self-regulation of the professions.

If a national anti-corruption strategy is a by-product of the experience of judicial tribunals of inquiry, it must recognise that (a) corruption is a constant danger, and (b) *ad hoc* tribunals are an expensive and cumbersome instrument to counter the threat. A state anti-corruption agency should be considered to monitor and diagnose signs of corruption. Such a body could also receive information from citizens, businesses, public employees and others with the protection of anonymity. It could highlight areas vulnerable to corruption and inform the oversight of the Dáil, the gardaí and other regulatory agencies. Unlike the Public Offices Commission, such a body would undertake investigations on the basis of passive indicators of corruption as well as complaints and referrals. It should also cover local government, health boards and other public sector organisations where discretion, while necessary, is open to abuse. A state anti-corruption agency could be created relatively quickly by extending the terms of the Standards in Public Office Bill, 2000.

Local or 'Citizen' Level Strategies

Most citizens' interaction with the state is at local level. In Ireland there is no expectation that bribes are required to obtain or facilitate services from local authority, state or related agencies. Despite very infrequent cases of fraud, Irish bureaucracy is not extractive or arbitrary. As suggested in Chapter Four, corruption in local government, outside planning, is incidental. Even when citizens seek the intervention of politicians, no money or favours are exchanged. Further, quite contrary to the assertion of Bax,[9] recruitment and promotion within the public service are based on merit criteria. Promotion for public servants does not necessitate political support. The explanation for the clientelist system in Ireland revolves around differing interests and understanding of policy.[10]

In other jurisdictions, corruption has been a major problem which threatens public confidence in the police. Officers, when based for a long time in one place, were seen as at risk of corruption. For example, in America the old-fashioned beat cop was viewed as in the path of constant temptation as compared to officers dispatched centrally in cars who did not spend much time in any one place. Similarly, low pay was seen as a reason for police corruption. In Ireland, as elsewhere, drug dealers can afford to offer huge sums to police officers to look the other way or be somewhere else when a deal is being done. Despite the very infrequent rogue garda, most Irish people have regarded the police force as a pillar of society. Recent cases of disquiet in Donegal and elsewhere have, however, put a strain on the system under which allegations of corrupt practices are examined by an internal Garda investigation.

Local anti-corruption strategies need to recognise that the major source of disquiet at a local level is planning, which demands national action. Significantly, the Local Government Bill 2000 provides for a strict ethics framework for councillors and local authority staff especially in relation to planning. In most other areas of service delivery, priority should be given to increasing the consumer orientation of public services. For such strategies to work, it is also important to acknowledge the role of elected representatives as a source of consumer response.[11] It is unlikely that the pattern of Irish clientelism will alter in the short term. Anti-corruption strategies should acknowledge the interest elected members will show in individual cases as opposed to general policy.

This consumer orientation would translate into actions to:

- increase access to services;
- widen choice of services and providers;
- improve information;
- make clearer the means of redress; and,
- introduce systematic testing of consumers' opinions.

Many of these reforms are in train under the SMI and new local government structures such as the strategic policy committees. Similarly, the new mayoral system will bring greater clarity to local accountability.

Populist strategies

> There will be no end to large-scale tax dodging and corruption . . . until the culprits are jailed . . . [T]he general public cannot be convinced that things have changed on foot of the tribunal and other inquiry revelations until they see somebody guilty of wrongdoing going to jail . . . [O]ur prisons are still seen as working class institutions and white collar crime is not seen as real crime. It's time people like auditors, bankers and other professionals who collude in things like tax dodging and other well off people who flout the law were made to pay the real price. (Deputy Jim Mitchell, Chair of the Dáil Public Accounts Committee, *Irish Examiner*, 17.7.00)

When discussing national strategies, much of the literature on corruption suggests that, as Deputy Mitchell advocates, success begins by 'frying a few big fish'. As Klitgaard et al. recommends:

> When there is a culture of engaging in corrupt acts with
> impunity, the only way to begin breaking it up is for a
> number of major corrupt figures to be convicted and
> punished. The government should quickly identify a few
> major tax evaders, a few big bribe givers, and a few
> high-level government bribe takers. Since a campaign
> against corruption can too often become a campaign
> against the opposition, the first big fish to be fried
> should be from the party in power.[12]

The scandal caused in the Republic by recent corruption may
persist despite the strategies suggested above. Popular opinion,
expressed, for instance, through by-elections, surveys and new
protest parties may require more dramatic demonstrative
actions. Nevertheless, in a highly politicised atmosphere, the
danger of star prosecutions is that they will distract attention
from the underlying causes of corruption. Indeed, the neo-
Marxist sociological model suggests that this is what such
actions are designed to do.

Conclusions

To an extent, according to Rose-Ackerman:

> Corruption scandals can then be a sign of a country's
> growing political maturity. They show that citizens are
> beginning to recognize the difference between the
> public and the private spheres and to complain when
> the border is crossed . . . that people recognize norms
> of fair dealing and competent administration . . .[13]

This is an optimistic view. It is, however, encouraged by an
analytical and international perspective. Domestic opinion in
most countries overestimates the extent of corruption. Where it
is tackled effectively, it is not attacked in isolation or by the criminal law alone. Populist measures may be necessary to garner
short-term public support and reassurance but they do not solve
the underlying problem. Further, as the Public Offices Commission points out in the context of the Ethics in Public Office Act

1995 and other anti-corruption legislation:

> The combined effects ... will ... contribute signifi-
> cantly, over time, to the development among politicians
> and public servants, in their dealings with business,
> with other important groups in Irish life and with the
> public generally, of standards of behaviour which
> should be beyond reproach ... [T]he concentration of
> the public debate on events which occurred before the
> passing of this legislation and the establishment of the
> Commission has tended to diminish what has been
> achieved and to result in a lack of recognition of the
> changes which have taken place.[14]

An anti-corruption strategy for the Republic should take into
account a realistic assessment of the problem and progress to
date. In the broadest terms, it should recognise the core
concerns that have been highlighted by the recent tribunals,
especially the interaction of the public and private sectors in
areas of policy discretion. Corruption is not simply an issue for
politicians and public officials. Further, strategies need to incor-
porate methods for evaluating the effectiveness of the measures
taken. In this context, passive indicators should be developed as
a form of early warning system.

Corruption is likely to be an issue in the Republic for the next
general election. It is important for continued popular support
that anti-corruption strategies have some tangible success as
quickly as possible.

6. Conclusions

The definition of corruption as the abuse of a public role for a
private benefit is widely accepted though it should be seen as
including instances where the gain is as much partisan as
personal. There is much less agreement in the academic literature on the nature and causes of corruption. Some of the
disagreement is a product of the analytical framework favoured.

Thus, public choice theorists prefer the economic models that draw so directly on the idea of rent seeking. They are particularly influential in the policy recommendations as well as the weight of research output from the World Bank. There is a rigorous logic to this approach that is attractive in its all-embracing compass. This model deserves its prominence. It takes, however, too simplistic a view of the motives of politicians, officials and citizens to be entirely persuasive, particularly to understand corruption in the context of local culture and history. Similarly, the economic approach does not easily account for uneven patterns of corruption within and between institutions. Further, it does not allow for the influence of a public service ethic, the democratic development or personal moral conviction. In Ireland, it is clear that, while the seachange accounts may be flawed, idealism has played some role both in keeping corruption in check both historically and now.

The models of corruption favoured by many political scientists have stressed the traditional pluralist virtues of civic society i.e. competitive elections, pressure groups interaction, a neutral role for the state, attentive citizens and vigorous parliamentary supervision of the executive. Unsurprisingly, this outlook dominates much of the policy perspectives of American-based non-governmental organisations such as the National Democratic Institute. It alerts the analyst to look for factors that inhibit the political efficacy of citizens, freedom of the press and separation of powers. Unfortunately, the recent experience of several liberal democracies, which have all the pluralist features above and more, is rather discouraging. Nevertheless, with the possible exception of Italy, no established liberal democracy is systemically corrupt.

The approach to corruption in Ireland adopted in this study has sought to draw on each of the models discussed above as well as insights from sociology and anthropology. It has, however, adopted a relatively long-term perspective to see corruption as grounded in the Republic's post-independence experience. This approach has suggested the likelihood of corruption in the early decades of the state for which there is little direct evidence. This is not because, as with economic models, it assumes only motives of self-interest. Certain public policies and institutional arrangements, however, have an association with corruption elsewhere in similar circumstances and valid questions can be asked of Ireland's experience. The model is essentially comparative. In making comparisons, however, this study has sought to draw lessons for Ireland from other newly formed states by using the literature on corruption in developing countries. This literature also has the advantage of drawing in the role of international actors that are frequently ignored in other models. Ireland is not the recipient of significant foreign aid but EU transfers, multinational investment and foreign trade are all important.

The main distinctions made in the literature between incidental and institutional corruption, the two most relevant

TABLE 6.1: Differing Features in both Relevant Forms of Corruption

	Incidental	Institutional
Frequency	Episodic	Routine
Level	One or few persons	Narrow but pervasive
Controls	Generally sufficient	Weak
Public trust	Generally high	Low

categories for Ireland, revolve around the characteristics summarised in Table 6.1.

This study has looked primarily at what has elsewhere been called 'grand corruption', which is mostly practised by elites. It categorises Ireland as institutionally corrupt, i.e. there is reason to suspect that in certain areas corruption is routine and pervasive. By the nature of corruption, such an assessment is both dated and tentative. If it is accurate, however, certain steps need to be taken and these are described in general terms in the suggested anti-corruption strategies outlined in Chapter Five.

There have been no proven cases of corruption involving urban renewal, tax exemptions, telephone licences and other areas of policy discretion, but some past decisions may still have to be revisited. Similarly, the judicial branch of government may have to become more obviously beyond suspicion.

Incidental corruption is present in all states though it is probably encouraged by the experience of the more serious category. In terms of the model used here, the conclusion of the analysis is that corruption in the Republic, while not systemic, is institutional:

- it is routine in some areas;
- in these, it occurs pervasively;
- weak or lax controls are associated with it; and,
- public trust in these areas is low.

In particular, it has been found where:

- politicians have a direct role in deciding specific, individual policy decisions of high value to wealthy business interests such as planning at local government level;
- civil servants routinely exercise discretion over commercially valuable decisions in the context of lax systems of accountability and ambiguous policy objectives; and,
- ministerial decisions are both commercially charged and the policy criteria are insufficiently explicit.

Combating corruption in Ireland is in part a matter of faith in the strength of the tradition of representative democracy. It is necessary that, despite examples of corruption among parliamentarians, the legislature is part of the solution rather than the problem. The Dáil must affirm its commitment to principles of integrity to regain the public's trust. It might do this by setting out in simple and accessible terms a code of conduct for its members. Such a code would be aspirational but, by adhering to it, politicians could demonstrate ethical leadership. There are already encouraging signs that existing laws are to be toughened and new legislation introduced. No one measure will bring corruption under control, but by understanding its dynamics, the Irish political system could be structured to reduce both its incidence and impact.

Notes and References

INTRODUCTION

1   Klitgaard, R., *International Co-operation Against Corruption,* (1997), Internet Center for Corruption Research Goettingen University (http://www.gwdg.de/~uwvw/research.htm.)

2   Jonson, M., 'Comparing Corruption: Conflicts, Standards and Development', paper at the XVI World Congress of the International Political Science Association, Berlin, 1994

1. UNDERSTANDING CORRUPTION IN IRISH POLITICS

1   Fiorentini, G. and Zamagni, S. (eds.) *The Economics of Corruption and Illegal Markets* (Cheltenham: Edward Elgar, 1999)

2   della Porta, D. and Vannucci, A., 'The "Perverse Effects" of Political Corruption', *Political Studies,* Vol. 45, 1997, pp. 516–38

3   Cartier-Bresson, J., 'The Economics of Corruption', in D. della Porta and M. Yves, *Democracy and Corruption in Europe* (London: Pinter, 1997), p. 153

4   Hussein Syed A., *Corruption: its nature, causes and functions* (Aldershot: Avebury, 1990), p. 154

5   Rose-Ackerman, S., *Corruption and Government* (Cambridge University Press, 1999), p. 99

6   Robson, T., *The state and community action* (London: Pluto Press, 2000)

7   Tanzi, V., *Policies, Institutions and the Dark Side of Economics* (Cheltenham: Edward Elgar, 2000), p. 91

8   ibid., p. 92

9   Riley, S.P., 'The Political Economy of Anti-Corruption Strategies in Africa', in M. Robinson (ed.) *Corruption and Development* (London: Frank Cass, 1998), p. 139

10   ibid., p. 139

11   Klitgaard, R., 'Cleaning Up and Invigorating the Civil Service', Report for the Operations Evaluation Department (Washington DC: World Bank, 1997)

12   Thornton, L. (1999) *Combating Corruption at the Grassroots: The Thailand Experience* (Washington DC: NDI, PI)

13   Geddes, B. and Ribeiro Neto, A., 'Institutional sources of corruption in Brazil', *Corruption and Political Reform in Brazil (*Coral Gables, Fla: North-South Center Press, 1999)

91

14　della Porta, D., 'Actors in corruption: Business Politicians in Italy', *International Social Science Journal*, vol. 149: 349–64, 1996, p. 19

15　Geddes, B. and Ribeiro Neto, A., 1999

16　Heywood, A., 'Political Corruption: Problems and Perspectives', *Political Studies,* vol. 45:3, 1997, p. 417

17　Galtung, F., 'Criteria for Sustainable Corruption Control', in M. Robinson (ed.) *Corruption and Development* (London: Frank Cass, 1998), pp. 105–28

18　Jain, A.K., *Economics of Corruption* (London: Kluwer Academic Publishers, 1998)

19　Geddes, B. and Ribeiro Neto, A., 1999, p. 23

20　Gallagher, M. and Komito, L., 'Dáil deputies and their constituency work', in J. Coakley and M. Gallagher (eds.), *Politics in the Republic of Ireland* (Limerick: PSAI Press, 1996), pp. 150–166

21　della Porta, D. and Vannucci, A., 1997, pp. 516–38

22　della Porta, D. and Vannucci, A., *Corrupt Exchanges: Actors, Resources and Mechanisms of Political Corruption* (New York: Aldine De Gruyter, 1999), p. 263

23　ibid., p. 261

24　ibid., pp. 258–9

25　ibid., p. 237

26　ibid., p. 67

27　For a fuller discussion of the role of the media see Sandroni, Claudia, 'Mediatized Politics and the Discourse of Political Corruption: a comparative analysis', unpublished MSc, University College Cork, 2000

2. CHRONICLING CORRUPTION IN IRISH POLITICS

1　Heywood, P., 'Political Corruption: Problems and Perspectives', *Political Studies* vol. XLV, 1997, p. 417

2　ibid., p. 419

3　FitzGerald, G., 'Long term honesty will pay', *The Irish Times*, 17.1.98

4　Dwyer, T.R., *Fallen Idol: Haughey's Controversial Career* (Cork: Mercier Press, 1997), p. 153

5　Hamilton, L., *Report of the Tribunal of Inquiry into the Beef Processing Industry* (Dublin: The Stationery Office, 1994)

6　McCracken, B., *Report of the Tribunal of Inquiry (Dunnes Payments)*, (Dublin: The Stationery Office, 1997)

7　http://www.moriarty-tribunal.ie

8   http://www.flood-tribunal.ie

9   *Magill*, 1.3.99

10 www.fiannafáil.ie (Report of the Committee on Standards in Public Life, June 2000)

11 Comptroller and Auditor General and Committees of the House of Oireachtas (Special Provisions) Act, 1999

12 Committee of Public Accounts, *Parliamentary inquiry into D.I.R.T.* (Dublin: Government of Ireland, 1999)

13 *Report of the Public Office Commission 1999* (Dublin: Stationery Office, 2000), p. 48

3. THE CAUSES OF CORRUPTION

1   Garvin, T., 'Democratic politics in independent Ireland', in John Coakley and Michael Gallagher (eds.), *Politics in the Republic of Ireland*, 3rd ed. (London: Routledge, 1999), p. 361

2   O'Leary, C., *Irish Elections 1918–1977* (Dublin: Gill and Macmillan, 1979), p. 42

3   Walsh, D., *Inside Fianna Fáil* (Dublin: Gill and Macmillan, 1986), p. 22

4   Maume, P., *The Long Gestation: Irish Nationalist Life 1891–1918*, (Dublin: Gill & Macmillan, 1999), p. 91

5   Garvin, T., *1922: The Birth of Irish Democracy* (Dublin: Gill and Macmillan, 1996), p. 65

6   *Local Appointments Commission, 1926–1976* (Dublin: Local Appointments Commission, 1976)

7   Munck, R., *The Irish Economy: Results and Prospects* (London: Pluto Press,1993), p. 30

8   Finnegan, R. and McCarron, E., *Ireland: Historical Echoes, Contemporary Politics* (Oxford: Westview Press, 2000), p. 93

9   Garvin, T., *The Evolution of Irish Nationalist Politics* (Dublin: Gill and Macmillan, 1981), p. 199

10   Keogh, D., *Twentieth-century Ireland: Nation and State* (Dublin: Gill and Macmillan, 1994)

11 Murphy, J.A., *Ireland in the Twentieth Century* (Dublin: Gill and Macmillan, 1977), p. 86

12 Dwyer, R., *The Examiner*, 20.2.99

13 ibid.

14 Coogan, T.P., *De Valera: Long Fellow, Long Shadow* (London: Hutchinson, 1993) p. 674

15   Hope, K.R., 'Corruption and Development in Africa', in K.R. Hope and B. Chicuto (eds.), *Corruption and Development in Africa: Lessons from Country Care Studies* (Basingstoke: Macmillan, 2000)

16   Robinson, M. (ed.), *Corruption and Development* (London: Frank Cass, 1998), p. 6

17   Collins, N. (ed.), *Political Issues in Ireland Today* (Manchester University Press, 1999)

18   Heywood, A., *Politics* (Basingstoke: Macmillan, 1997)

19   della Porta, D. and Vannucci, A., *Corrupt Exchanges: Actors, Resources and Mechanisms of Political Corruption* (New York: Adine de Gruyter, 1999), p. 115

20   ibid., p. 116

21   *The Examiner,* 13.11.99

22   *Evidence to the Dáil Public Accounts Committee,* 6.6.99

23   della Porta, D., 'Corruption and Democracy', *UNESCO Courier*, June 1996, p. 18

24   O'Higgins, E., 'Learning to recognise law and ethics divide', *The Irish Times*, 1.10.99

25   Johnson, M., 'Comparing Corruption: Conflicts, Standards and Development', paper at the XVI World Congress of the International Political Science Association, Berlin, 1994

26   Perry, P.J., *Political Corruption and Political Geography (*Brookfield, Vermount.: Ashgate, 1997)

27   Murtagh, P., *The Irish Times,* 16.11.99

28   Rose-Ackerman, S., *Corruption and Government* (Cambridge University Press, 1999)

29   Heywood, P., *Political Corruption* (Oxford: Blackwell, 1997), p. 14

30   Garvan, R. and Kelly, R., *British Politics Today* (Manchester University Press, 1998), p. 204

31   Butler, P. and Collins, N., 'Positioning Political Parties: A Market Analysis', *Harvard Journal of Press/Politics*, vol. 1(2), 1996, pp. 63–77

32   Heywood, P., 'Continuity and Change: Analysing Political Corruption in Modern Spain', in Walter Little and Eduardo Posada-Carbo (eds.), *Political Corruption in Europe and Latin America* (New York: St. Martin's Press, 1996), p. 15

33   Browne, V., 'Not merely individuals but parties are for sale', *The Irish Times,* 3.3.99

34   Masterson, E., *Ireland on Sunday*, 27.2.00

35   della Porta, D. and Vannucci, A., 1999

36   Geddes, B. and Ribeiro Neto, A., 'Institutional sources of corruption in Brazil', *Corruption and Political Reform in Brazil* (Coral Gables, Fla: North-South Center Press, 1999), p. 33

37   ibid., p. 35

38   della Porta, D. and Vannucci, A., 'The "Perverse Effects" of Political Corruption', *Political Studies*, vol. 45, 1997, p. 516

39   Masterson, E., *Ireland on Sunday*, 27.2.00

40   O'Sullivan, M.C., 'The Social and Political Characteristics of the Twenty-eight Dáil', in M. Marsh and P. Mitchell (eds.), *How Ireland Voted 1997* (Oxford: Westview Press, 1999), p. 1187

41   della Porta, D. and Pizzorno, A., 'The Business Politicians: Reflections from a Study on Political Corruption', *Journal of Law and Society*, 1996

42   Heywood, P., 'Political Corruption: Problems and Perspectives', *Political Studies*, vol. 45, no.3,1997, pp. 417–35

43   Rose-Ackerman, S., 1999, p. 133

44   della Porta, D., 'Corruption and Democracy', *UNESCO Courier*, June 1996, p. 18

45   della Porta, D., 1996, p. 19

46   Donnelly, S., *Elections '97* (Dublin: Sean Donnelly, 1998)

47   della Porta, D., 1996

4. THE CONSEQUENCES OF CORRUPTION IN IRELAND

1   Hope, K.R., 'Corruption and Development in Africa', in K.R. Hope and B. Chicuto (eds.), *Corruption and Development in Africa: Lessons from Country Care Studies* (Basingstoke: Macmillan, 2000)

2   Wolf, M., *Financial Times*, 16.8.97

3   Shang-Jin, Wei, 'Corruption in Economic Development: Beneficial Grease, Minor Annoyance, or Major Obstacle?' (Washington: Word Bank, Working Paper Series, 1999)

4   Soros, G., *The Crisis of Global Capitalism* (London: Little, Brown and Company, 1998)

5   Wolf, M., *Financial Times*, 16.8.97

6   Johnston, M., 'The Political Costs of Corruption', paper at *Primera Conferencia Latinoamericana de Lucha Contra La Corrupcion Administrativa*, p. 12

7   Lambsdroff, J.G., 'Corruption in Empirical. A review', *Transparency International 1999*, p. 54.

8   Johnston, M., 1993, p. 5

9   Held, D., *Models of Democracy*, (Cambridge: Polity Press, 1996)

10   McAllister, I., 'Keeping them Honest: Public and Elite Perceptions of Ethical Conduct among Australian Legislators', *Political Studies*, vol. 48, 2000, p. 23

11   Buckley, F., 'Non-voting in Ireland', paper given to the PSAI Post-graduate Conference, Dublin, 2000

12   della Porta, D. and Vannucci, A., *Corrupt exchanges: actors, resources and mechanisms of political corruption* (New York: Adine de Gruyter, 1999), p. 103

13   http://www.transparency.de/documents/pressreeases/2000/2000.03.08. womensday.html See also Dollar, David, 'Are women really the fairer sex? Corruption and Women in Government', reprinted in *World Bank Policy Research Report on Gender and Development,* Working Paper Series, No. 4; Eckel and Grossman 'Are women less selfish than men? Evidence from dictator games', *The Economic Journal 1996 and 1998*; Swamy, 'Gender and corruption', IRIS Center Working Paper, University of Maryland, 1999

14   Heywood, P., 'Political Corruption: Problems and Perspectives', *Political Studies,* vol. 45, no. 3, 1997, p. 419

15   Geddes B. and Ribeiro Neto, A., 'Institutional sources of corruption in Brazil', *Corruption and Political Reform in Brazil* (Coral Gables, Fla: North-South Center Press, 1999) p. 43

16   McAllister, I., 2000 p. 25

17   *Bunreacht na hEireann*: 15.13 (1937)

18   National Democratic Institute for International Affairs, 'Legislative Ethics: a Comparative Analysis', Legislative Research Series Paper #4, (Washington: National Democratic Institute for International Affairs, 1999) p. 17

19   FitzGerald, G., 'Agreements depart from traditional democracy', *The Irish Times,* 12.2.00

5. ANTI-CORRUPTION STRATEGIES

1   Klitgaard, R., *Institutional Adjustment and Adjusting to Institutions*, World Bank Discussion Paper No. 303, 1995, p. 32

2   Tanzi, V., *Policies, Institutions and the Dark Side of Economics,* (Cheltenham: Edward Elgar, 2000) p. 130

3   OECD, *Public Sector Corruption: an international survey of prevention measures* (Paris: OECD, 2000)

4   Riley, S.P., 'The Political Economy of Anti-Corruption Strategies in Africa', in M. Robinson (ed.), *Corruption and Development* (London: Frank Cass, 1998)

5   http://www.oecd.org//daf//nocorruption

6   http://www.oecd.org/daf/nocorruption.faq.htm

7   *European Voice*, (28.6.00)

8   *Sunday Independent*, editorial, 9.7.00

9   Bax, M., *Harpstrings and confessions: machine-style politics in the Irish Republic* (Assen: Van Gorcum, 1976)

10   Collins, N., *Local Government Managers at Work* (Dublin: Institute of Public Administration, 1987)

11   Patrick, B., and Collins, N., 'Embracing the Cute Hoors: reassessing the role of politicians in the delivery of public services', paper to the 'Management in the 21st Century', Irish Academy of Management Conference, Dublin, 2000

12   Klitgaard, R., MacLean-Abaroa, R. and Lindsey Parris, H., *Corrupt Cities: A Practical Guide to Cure and Prevention* (Washington: World Bank, 2000) p. 72

13   Rose-Ackerman, S., *Corruption and Government* (Cambridge University Press, 1999) p. 225

14   Annual Report of the Public Offices Commission, 1999

Bibliography

Bax, M. (1976) *Harpstrings and Confessions: Machine-style Politics in the Irish Republic*, (Assen: Van Gorcum)

Collins, N. ed. (1999) *Political Issues in Ireland Today*, (Manchester: Manchester University Press)

della Porta, D. and Vannucci, A. (1999) *Corrupt Exchanges: Actors, Resources and Mechanisms of Political Corruption*, (New York: Adine de Gruyter)

della Porta, D. and Yves, M. (1997) *Democracy and Corruption in Europe*, (London: Pinter)

Garvin, T. (1996) *1922: The Birth of Irish Democracy*, (Dublin: Gill & Macmillan)

Garvin, T. (1981) *The Evolution of Irish Nationalist Politics*, (Dublin: Gill & Macmillan)

Geddes, B. and Ribeiro Neto, A. (1999) *Corruption and Political Reform in Brazil*, (Coral Gables, Fla: North-South Center Press)

Held, D. (1996) *Models of Democracy*, (Cambridge: Polity Press)

Hope, K. and Chicuto, B. (eds), *Corruption: Its Nature, Causes and Functions*, (Avebury: Aldershot) p. 154

Jain, A.K. (1998) *Economics of Corruption*, (London: Kluwer Academic Publishers)

Keogh, D. (1994) *Twentieth-Century Ireland: Nation and State*, (Dublin: Gill & Macmillan)

Klitgaard, R. (1997) 'Cleaning Up and Invigoration the Civil Service', A Report for the Operations Evaluation Department, (Washington, DC: World Bank)

Klitgaard, R. MacLean-Abaroa, R. and Lindsey Parris, H. (2000) *Corrupt Cities: A Practical Guide to Cure and Prevention*, (Washington, DC: World Bank)

Lambsdroff, J.G. (1999) 'Corruption in Empirical: A Review', Transparency International

Robinson, M. (ed) *Corruption and Development*, (London: Frank Cass)

Robson, T. (2000) *The State and Community Action*, (London: Pluto Press)

Rose-Ackerman, S. (1999) Corruption and Government, (Cambridge: Cambridge University Press)

Sandroni, C. (2000) 'Mediatized Politics and the Discourse of Political Corruption: a comparative analysis' (MSc Thesis, University College Cork)

Tanzi, V. (2000) *Policies, Institutions and the Dark Side of Economics*, (Cheltenham: Edward Elgar)